2/18/16

Alliance for Defending
Freedom

1) Necessity of Religious
2) Sanctity of life
3) Sanctity of Marriage

Brothers, Stand Firm

Brothers, Stand Firm

Seven Things Every Man Should Know,
Practice, and Invest in the Next Generation

Steve Bateman

WIPF & STOCK · Eugene, Oregon

BROTHERS, STAND FIRM
Seven Things Every Man Should Know, Practice, and Invest in the Next Generation

Wipf and Stock
An Imprint of Wipf and Stock Publishers
199 W. 8th Ave., Suite 3
Eugene, OR 97401

www.wipfandstock.com

ISBN 13: 978-1-62564-684-2

Manufactured in the U.S.A.   11/11/2014

Unless otherwise noted, all Scripture is from the ESV.

To Josh and Sean, my son and son-in-law,
who have been called to stand firm in "such a time as this."

Contents

CONTENTS

Acknowledgments

THIS BOOK IS A tribute to all the manly mentors in my life who have for decades stood firm in their allegiance to Jesus Christ. Their hair is grayer. Their bodies are weaker. Their course is nearly done. By their example of competence and character, they have inspired me to finish this race well. You know who you are.

This book for men would not be possible without a few key women. First and foremost, my wonderful bride Lori has been my main encourager throughout the long and arduous process that is writing a book. I wanted to quit. She didn't want me to. She won. My daughter, Joy, was single when I started writing this book, and she and her friends affirmed my conviction that the church has a shortage of strong young men filled with Christian courage. Yet, by God's grace, she found such a man (in our church!) before the book was completed. This book is a much better book because of the wise suggestions of my friend, experienced author and skilled theologian, Susan Hunt. And many thanks to Cynthia McPherson who did the copy-editing on this book and does so well the things I like the least: formatting and footnotes!

The book's cover is the creative concept of Joel McWhorter, a long-time friend, hunting partner, church member, deacon, and co-laborer at First Bible Church. This is not the first time he has given his talent to the cause of Christ. Also, Vance Helms, my colleague and Pastor of Discipleship at First Bible Church, has helped me a great deal with the discussion questions that are found at this book's website www.7things.org.

Finally, I wrote this book for the men of First Bible Church. For over two decades in this place my priority has been to entrust these seven things "to faithful men who will be able to teach others also." By God's grace, we have an abundance of faithful men in this church. Now, Brothers, stand firm!

—— Introduction ——
Brothers, Stand Firm

CAMPING IN THE SNOW sounds like fun until you actually do it. As darkness falls, there is nothing to do except stare at a fire. Halfway through the night, you feel like you will never be warm again. Morning cannot come soon enough.

On Christmas Day in 1776, George Washington and the Continental Army had experienced their fill of winter camping. In the warmth of spring, the Americans had pushed British troops out of Boston. In the balm of summer, they took control of New York. In the heady days of July, the Founders signed the Declaration of Independence. A new nation was born.

By late August, however, a reinforced British army had ousted the Americans from New York, and Washington led his troops in a strategic withdrawal. In early December, they crossed the Delaware River and made camp in the fields of Pennsylvania. Long before waterproof boots, moisture-wicking clothes, and down-filled coats, they were cold, tired, and, above all, scared.

Fear is contagious. Cowardice is caught. Discouragement is infectious. Every morning, American troops woke to find more empty places around the campfire. In the middle of night, their brothers-in-arms ran from the fight, abandoned their posts, and headed for the soft comforts of home. Desertions were high and morale was low as the cause of the American Revolution hung by a thread.

On December 23, 1776, Washington gathered his men and read a recently published essay penned by Thomas Paine, beginning with those familiar and stirring words:

> These are the times that try men's souls. The summer soldier and the sunshine patriot will, in this crisis, shrink from the service of his country; but he who stands by it now deserves the love and thanks of man and woman.[1]

1. Paine, "American Crisis," 135.

Two days later, in the bitter cold of Christmas Day evening, Washington led his troops in one of the most audacious maneuvers in the history of war. After crossing the icy Delaware River, they attacked the unsuspecting Hessian troops at Trenton, New Jersey, and won a resounding victory.

Is This Our Trenton?

There are pivotal moments in history when the trajectory of marriages, families, businesses, movements, and nations could go one way or the other, producing very different outcomes. Many Americans are unaware of how close the United States came to meeting an abrupt end in its infancy. The Battle of Trenton, historians agree, was a turning point. Had it gone the other way, we must imagine a world without the United States.

For two thousand years the church at different times, serving in different nations, pressured by different cultures, has faced its own Trentons. Church history is the record of the gospel advancing in one generation, only to give up ground in the next. It is no accident that the Bible speaks of this struggle as war.

At the end of his life, the Apostle Paul invited Timothy to "share in suffering as a good soldier of Jesus Christ" (2 Tim 2:3) and could say, "I have fought the good fight" (2 Tim 4:7). For Paul, a partner in the gospel was a "fellow soldier" (Phil 2:25). Likewise, Jude commands disciples of Jesus to "contend for the faith that was once for all delivered to the saints" (Jude 3).

This war is not against "flesh and blood, but against the . . . spiritual forces of evil in the heavenly places" (Eph 6:12). Our weapons are not swords, or guns, or bombs, or fear, but the loving and persuasive proclamation of the Word of God, which is "sharper than any two-edged sword" (Heb 4:12). Our enemy, the devil (Matt 13:39), is against everything that God is for. He seeks to undo what God does, divide what God unites, and tear down what God builds up. You have an enemy who is committed to your destruction. He wants your life. He wants your wife. He wants your kids.

This enemy is a created and fallen being, more powerful than you, but weaker than God. So he focuses his limited resources on strategic targets. And you are a strategic target.

The enemy knows that if he can take out husbands and fathers, he can dismantle families. If he dismantles families, he destabilizes the church. If he destabilizes the church, the gospel will lose ground. Now, more than ever, the church needs men who will stand firm in the winter and take the fight to the enemy. The church needs no more summer soldiers or sunshine patriots.

The Situation in Thessalonica

Nearly two thousand years ago, the Apostle Paul wrote to a church that was losing ground. Thessalonica was a strategic port city and Paul labored to plant a church there, expecting these new disciples to carry the gospel to surrounding cities and villages. Things started well and these new believers became famous as word spread that they "turned to God from idols to serve the living and true God" (1 Thess 1:9). That kind of victory attracted the attention of the enemy who activated a two-pronged campaign he still uses today.

First, he attacks from the outside. That is, he will tempt unbelievers, especially those who hold religious or political power, to persecute the church. Acts 17 describes how Paul captured territory for God's glory in Thessalonica through persuasive preaching. Immediately, religious and political authorities physically attacked the new church leaders and unjustly charged them with crimes against Caesar. These new believers were tempted to remain silent and deny Christ in order to protect their social status, financial assets, and political influence.

Second, he attacks from the inside. That is, he seduces people to doubt and distort the Word of God and infiltrate the church to influence others. Jesus had warned that many would come in his name claiming to speak for him, but they would "lead many astray" (Matt 24:5). In the case of the Thessalonians, false teachers had done just that. These religious leaders were claiming to speak for God, posing as apostles, and leading the church astray. For that reason, Paul warned the church: "let no one deceive you in any way" (2 Thess 2:3).

The attack may be external, coming in the form of verbal, physical, or political persecution from outside the church. Or the attack may be internal, coming in the form of eloquent, convincing, smooth-talking religious leaders inside the church. Either way, Paul writes to the Thessalonian believers to arm them so they can defend the faith in trying circumstances. Like Washington at Trenton, he exhorts them in an attempt to boost their morale:

> So then, brothers, stand firm and hold to the traditions that you were taught by us, either by our spoken word or by our letter (2 Thess 2:15).

He calls them brothers because they are in the family of God. The Greek word here, *adelphoi*, literally means "from the same womb," so it does not always refer only to males. It can be used in the generic sense of siblings. Because they received Christ, both men and women were adopted into the family of God, who became their heavenly Father. Genuine Christians are brothers and sisters in Christ who fight this enemy together, but as is the case in every war in all of history, men are expected to lead the way and spill the most blood in a just cause.

Standing is the posture of a soldier in battle. When he falls to the ground, he is at a disadvantage. When he runs from the fight, he puts the mission at risk, betrays the cause, and demoralizes his fellow soldiers. This is no time for breezy carelessness. This is the time for situational awareness. This is no time to retreat. This is the time to hold your ground, and as Paul told the Corinthians, "be watchful, stand firm in the faith, act like men, be strong" (1 Cor 16:13).

What soldier goes into battle unarmed? In his hands he tightly grips the teaching of the apostles. "Tradition" refers to a body of treasured truth that is transferred from one person to another, from one generation to the next. So Paul tells them to hold to the traditions that he taught them, either face to face or by letter. For example, he had already sent them 1 Thessalonians. This letter is not just a word from Paul, but "a word from the Lord" (1 Thess 4:15). True Christians will affirm what the apostles affirm and deny what the apostles deny. That's what the church has done from the very beginning, when the earliest Christians "devoted themselves to the apostles' teaching" (Acts 2:42).

Brothers, stand firm and strongly hold to the sound teaching of the Word of God. The Bible is your sword (Eph 6:17) and you must master certain skills to use it well. Stand firm, because all around you, sunshine soldiers—professing Christians who wore the uniform in the parades of sunnier days—are surrendering that sword, turning their backs to the battle, and slipping away in the cover of night.

The Challenge for This Generation

Most chapters in this book begin with a quote from a well-known American who was raised in what most would call a Christian home. Many of them went to Sunday school, several were active in their church youth groups, and a few were PKs—preachers' kids. By cultural standards, they are successful people, some achieving staggering amounts of fame and fortune. Yet they have all either rejected Christianity or the church of their childhood or practice a religion that would not be recognized by the apostles as Christian. I cannot make any judgments about their parents or the church they were raised in, one way or the other. All I know is that they believe they have heard the Christian message, understood it, and, for a variety of reasons, found it lacking.

Sadly, their stories are not unusual. At every turn, this defection is both lamented and praised, but few deny that it is happening. For those who hate the church, this is good news because Christianity loses its dominant influence on our nation's culture, laws, and policies. For those who love the church, there is a broken-hearted grief as the name of Jesus is besmirched and the culture spirals downward in moral confusion. There seems to be no end to the books and blogs addressing this alarming trend, and no shortage of theories to explain the decline. Surveys are conducted, polls are taken, focus groups are assembled, and twenty-somethings are asked, "Why did you leave the church?" The responses seem to be all over the map: The church is too judgmental, too shallow, too outdated, too anti-science, too anti-intellectual, too anti-women, too anti-gay, too political, too sexually repressive, too arrogant, too irrelevant, too intolerant, too exclusive, or just plain too uncool.

The church's failure to be a more beautiful bride of Christ is not the only explanation. Our children are growing up in a youth-glorifying culture that has infected them in more ways than we can know. Consequently, children, teenagers, and emerging adults today are often too selfish, too narcissistic, too self-indulged, too fixated on their self-esteem, too coddled, too pampered, too soft, too fat, too enamored with peer approval, too entitled, too naïve, too self-absorbed, and just plain too cool. If being cool is your goal, Jesus' summons to come and die with him sounds like a stretch.

We would be naïve to think that Christians have never faced this challenge before. Over the centuries, Christian parents struggled against the culture and their own fallen nature to disciple their children. We are not the first generation to wonder and worry about our sons and daughters. We are not the first generation to ponder a perilous future for the church in America. The need of our generation is the same as every other: a disciplined army of credible men.

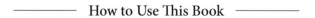

How to Use This Book

This book will be most helpful to you if you read it, think about it, agree with it, argue with it, and discuss it with other men in small groups. To help you do that, each chapter will end with a summary of things you should know in order to increase your competence. In addition, please visit www.7things.org to find a list of questions for each chapter to discuss with others in a small group. If you are a group leader, you can also download a free leader's guide at www.7things.org. If you are an individual reader studying this book on your own, the leader's guide is a great way to keep you focused.

---
 1 ───

Are We Losing This Generation?

At the end of the day, if there was indeed some body or presence standing there to judge me, I hoped I would be judged on whether I had lived a true life, not on whether I believed in a certain book, or whether I'd been baptized.

−LANCE ARMSTRONG[1]

The deplorable conditions which I recently encountered when I was a visitor constrained me to prepare this brief and simple catechism or statement of Christian teaching. Good God, what wretchedness I beheld! . . . Although the people are supposed to be Christian, are baptized, and receive the holy sacrament, they do not know the Lord's prayer, the Creed, or the Ten Commandments.

−MARTIN LUTHER, PREFACE TO LUTHER'S SMALL CATECHISM, 1529[2]

ONE OF THE MOST famous and disgraced athletes in the history of sport is adamantly opposed to biblical Christianity. While our Heisman Trophy and Cy Young winners are famous in the United States, they are anonymous beyond our borders. However, at least one American athlete has been loved and hated in both North America and Europe. As the seven-time winner of the Tour de France, Lance Armstrong knew what it was like to sit on the throne of the cycling world. His name recognition won him a host of endorsement deals, from beer to bikes to power bars. One thing he never endorsed was a life of following Jesus Christ.

1. Armstrong, *It's Not about the Bike.*
2. Unless otherwise noted, all quotations from Christian creeds, confessions, and catechisms are from Pelikan and Hotchkiss, *Creeds and Confessions of Faith.*

As a cancer survivor, Lance Armstrong knows what it's like to stare death in the face. He also knows what it is like to contemplate what's on the other side. One night in his hospital room, he envisioned how a conversation with the Almighty will go:

> If there was indeed a god at the end of my days I hoped he didn't say, "But you were never a Christian so you're going the other way from heaven." If so, I was going to reply, "You know what? You're right. Fine." [3]

You get the sense there is something in the back story that explains this designer religion we might call "Lancianity." It's a mixture of wishful thinking and brash defiance with a dose of anger thrown in. Born and raised in the Bible Belt and exposed to Christianity at a young age, Lance chose to reject it. Why? We'll get to that later, but for now, it is important to realize he is not alone as the generation behind him follows his deadly lead.

The Generation That Is Getting Away

A decade's worth of extensive surveys has produced a massive body of evidence that should alarm anyone concerned about the future of Christianity in America. Startling numbers of teenagers and young adults in the church are not keeping the faith. While every study varies, they all agree on four things.

First, the beliefs of young Americans who were raised in Christian homes have significantly departed from the historic Christian faith, while "only a minority of American teens appear to be 'bible literate.'" [4] In a landmark longitudinal study, Christian Smith, Professor of Sociology at Notre Dame, concludes that as American teenagers are moving into their early twenties, they are "souls in transition," and many are moving away from the church. Even those "emerging adults" (ages 18–23) who grew up in churches described as conservative Protestant confessed to some troubling beliefs. Only 64 percent of them believe that only people whose sins are forgiven through faith in Jesus Christ will go to heaven. Forty-five percent believe that many religions other than Christianity may be true, so it is not surprising that 40 percent of conservative Protestant teenagers believe it

---

3. Armstrong, *It's Not about the Bike*.
4. Wachlin, "What do American Teens."

is okay for them to practice other religions besides their own.[5] "The overall story," writes Smith, "is clearly one of general religious decline among youth transitioning from the teenage years into the emerging adulthood."[6]

Second, the ethics of young Americans raised in Christian homes are often barely distinguishable from those who were raised in non-Christian homes. Today's emerging adults largely determine right from wrong by how they feel. Moral authority is found within them, not outside of them in some objective standard such as the Bible. Even if they say they believe the Bible, many of them see the Scripture as a rough guideline that must submit to the authority of their own sovereign emotions. All the religions of the world can be cherry-picked as individuals select the moral teachings in each that help them live better lives, fit into their own experience, and make them feel good about themselves. They feel free to leave out everything else they do not like. In the end, they live by the moral code of "What Seems Right to Me."[7]

It follows then, that the less they attend church, pray, and read the Bible the more likely they are to binge drink, do drugs, neglect the poor and elderly, view pornography, have oral sex with casual partners, and have unmarried sexual intercourse. Sixty-one percent of the college students in our own congregations are sexually active, admitting they have had sexual intercourse within the last thirty days.[8]

Third, the church attendance of young Americans raised in Christian homes is in decline. Among conservative Protestants in their early twenties, 28 percent attend every Sunday while 24 percent never participate in public worship at all. That leaves about half of them to attend church whenever they feel like it. And often in the college years, they don't much feel like it.[9]

Isn't this just a normal event for college students? Haven't they always slacked off of church attendance during the college years only to return afterwards? When they get married and start having children, surely they'll settle down and get back to church, right?

5. These numbers could be worse, and in many churches they are. For example, according to Smith, among emerging adults from *mainline* Protestant churches, only 59 percent believe in the deity and physical resurrection of Jesus, and just 33 percent believe that faith in him is the only way to heaven. Not surprisingly, six out of ten say they never read the Bible.

6. Smith, *Souls in Transition*, 118.

7. Ibid., 156–57.

8. Ibid., 257–78.

9. Ibid., 116.

Some of them do return, but increasingly, more stay away for several reasons. First, they are delaying marriage and parenthood. The average age for marriage in 1970 was 22 while today it is 27, if they get married at all. American culture now extends adolescence far beyond the bounds of previous generations, enabling for many a party-college lifestyle well into their twenties. The longer they stay away from the church, the less likely it is that they will come back. In fact, one third of college-aged conservative Protestants do not expect to be attending church when they are 30 years old.[10]

Fourth, and especially troubling, fewer young adults who were raised in church see the importance of marrying a Christian. Just 39 percent of conservative Protestants responded that it was extremely or very important to marry someone of their own religion.[11] Scripture repeatedly warns believers against marrying unbelievers,[12] yet these warnings are largely ignored. Husbands and wives are exhorted to work together in a holy partnership, raising up the next generation for God's glory,[13] so a Christian's first criterion for a marriage partner should be an unapologetic commitment to Christ. If that standard is not in place, the future of vibrant Christianity is, humanly speaking, in jeopardy.

A Lesson from Lance Armstrong's Father

I cannot emphasize this point enough: teaching the next generation requires more than a transfer of biblical knowledge. It also requires an authentic, valiant, Spirit-empowered application of biblical knowledge to your own life.

The fall of Lance Armstrong is one of the most dramatic and heartbreaking in the history of sport. Stripped of his titles for the illegal use of performance-enhancing drugs, the requests for endorsements have ceased. Millions of promised dollars have now slipped through his hands. Friendships have been shattered. Trust has been destroyed. Sadly, the world now views him as a cheat and a liar, rich in athletic competence, but short on moral character.

Lance Armstrong never knew his biological father and still does not want to meet him. That man got his mother pregnant and then disappeared before Lance was two years old. When he was three, his mother married

10. Ibid., 140.
11. Ibid.
12. Deut 7:3–4; Ezra 10:2; 2 Cor 6:14; 1 Kgs 11:4.
13. Mal 2:15; Deut 6:7.

Terry Armstrong, who adopted him and gave him his name. "Terry Armstrong was a Christian," writes Armstrong, "and he came from a family who had a tendency to tell my mother how to raise me. But, for all of his proselytizing, Terry had a bad temper, and he used to whip me, for silly things. Kid things, like being messy."[14]

When Lance was a teenager, his mother underwent surgery. Instead of caring for her and being at her side in the hospital, Terry insisted on chaperoning Lance at a swim meet. "I didn't like it when he tried to play Little League Dad," he writes, "and I thought he should be at the hospital. But he insisted." And then something happened that forever fractured the tenuous bond between Lance and Terry Armstrong.

"As we sat in the airport waiting for our flight, I gazed at Terry and thought, *Why are you here?* As I watched him, he began to write notes on a pad. He would write, then ball up the paper and throw it into the garbage can and start again. I thought it was peculiar. After a while Terry got up to go to the bathroom. I went over to the garbage can, retrieved the wadded papers, and stuffed them into my bag. Later, when I was alone, I took them out and unfolded them. They were to another woman. I read them, one by one. He was writing to another woman while my mother was in the hospital having a hysterectomy."[15]

Lance Armstrong, arguably one of the best-known athletes in the history of sport, will be forever remembered as a liar and a cheat. Sadly, he grew up in the home of a man who was a professing Christian whom he accuses of being a liar and a cheat. And to this day, Lance Armstrong wants nothing to do with Christianity.

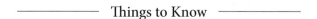 Things to Know

- What are the 4 ways this generation is departing from the historic Christian faith?

---

14. Armstrong, *It's Not about the Bike*, 20.

15. Ibid., 24. Lance Armstrong divorced his wife and the mother of his three children and moved in with singer Cheryl Crow in 2003. He has since left Crow and fathered two children with his girlfriend Anna Hansen.

2

Where Are the Men?

In my faith, you're just supposed to have faith, but I was always like—'Why?'...At this point, I'm just kind of a drifter. I'm open to possibility. My sponge is so big and wide and I'm soaking everything up and my mind has been radically expanded.

−KATY PERRY, RECORDING ARTIST, ACTRESS[1]

How will you bishops answer for it before Christ that you have so shamefully neglected the people and paid no attention at all to the duties of your office?... you do not take the slightest interest in teaching the people the Lord's Prayer, the Creed, the Ten Commandments, or a single part of the word of God. Woe to you forever!

−MARTIN LUTHER, PREFACE TO LUTHER'S SMALL CATECHISM, 1529

IF WE ARE NOT careful, we could despair, concluding that the decline of the church in America is inevitable, but the two greatest predictors of whether or not the children in our churches will keep the faith should strengthen our resolve.

First, the most powerful influence on a person's religious beliefs and practices is the parents. Most emerging adults see themselves as similar to their parents in terms of faith. There is no drastic rebellion or wholesale rejection of their parents' doctrine or ethics as they enter their twenties.[2] That can be bad news in that it may explain where young adults are getting most of their unsound doctrine and sloppy ethical thinking. However, it is good news in that parents still represent the most powerful human influence in a child's life.

1. Marikar, "Brad Pitt and More."
2. Smith, *Souls in Transition*, 129.

The second predictor that the church's sons and daughters will continue in the faith is active involvement in church life. *Specifically, if a teenager knows and is known by multiple adults, other than his or her parents, who personally love and live by the Bible, it is more likely that the teenager will love and live by the Bible.* These adults in the church serve as mentors who can "train them in the right believing and living of their faith."[3] It is impossible to measure, this side of heaven, the positive impact made by nursery workers, Sunday school teachers, youth pastors, and mission trip chaperones. The more of these adults there are in a child's life, the more likely the child will remain in church as he grows older.

Note that it is not just simple, ritualistic church attendance that made the difference, but rather the young person's sense of belonging (knowing and being known) in the church that is the most accurate predictor of church involvement later in life.

A Gospel Warning to Proud or Despairing Parents

There is no guarantee here and exceptions abound. Even the most consistent and godly parents may see a son or daughter turn away from Christ and his church. God is the only perfect Father, yet many of his children wander. It is a heart-broken God who declares "Children I have reared and brought up, but they have rebelled against me" (Isa 1:2). If it can happen to God, it can happen to us. On the other hand, even the most inconsistent and spiritually immature parents may see their children thrive in their walk with Christ and in church life. This usually happens because their children come under the influence of some other godly adults. If your children know, love, obey, and exalt Jesus Christ, that is only by the grace of God and you have no cause for boasting. If your children are far from God even though you have been faithful to teach and model the Christian faith, pray earnestly that, like the prodigal son in the famous story, they will see the insanity of eating pig food (Luke 15:16), but we would be naïve to think that parents make no difference.

Generally, but not certainly, the more serious parents are about their commitment to Jesus Christ and historic, apostolic Christianity, the more serious their children will be as well. Children who hear their parents earnestly teach the Bible and watch their parents consistently apply the Bible are more likely to continue in the Christian faith for the rest of their lives.

3. Ibid., 234.

"Parents matter most," writes Kenda Creasy Dean, Associate Professor of Youth, Church, and Culture at Princeton University, "when it comes to the religious formation of their children. While grandparents, other relatives, mentors, and youth ministers are also influential, parents are by far the most important predictors of teenagers' religious lives."[4]

And yet, as in all other things, parents must keep the gospel at the center of their parenting. In chapters 16–19, we will take an in-depth look at the gospel, but for now keep in mind that the gospel is the good news that Jesus Christ, the Son of God, died in the place of sinners (like you, me, and your children) and was raised from the dead in order to reconcile us to God. Those who receive the gospel are deeply, powerfully, and radically transformed, so that they will want to know, love, obey, and exalt Jesus Christ. Because God's justice is so firm, there is no hope for those who trust in their own righteousness, no matter the depth of their goodness. Because God's mercy is so deep, there is always hope for those who turn to Christ, no matter the depth of their sin. Nothing humbles the proud and comforts the despairing like the gospel.

We are not trying to raise little Pharisees. It is tempting to read a book like this in order to find out how to raise "nice" children who are well behaved and compliant, staying out of trouble and growing up to marry other "nice" people. We don't want our children to embarrass us in front of our friends. Forgetting the gospel and how God has treated us in Christ, we are tempted to manipulate our children, withholding our love when they fail, accepting them on the basis of their performance, motivating them with fear, guilt, and pride.

Surely, as parents we don't want our children to mess up their lives with the "big sins" that result in DUIs and unwanted pregnancies, but the answer is not moralism, focusing on outward conformity to God's laws to earn God's acceptance (and probably a parent's acceptance as well). While our children need to know God's moral standards, they also need to know they can never meet them because the hidden "little sins" are damnable too. That's why they need Jesus. Give them the gospel! The only person who ever met the moral standards of God died in the place of those of us who never will. It's possible for a child to be raised in a "Christian home" and never hear that it is only by the power of the gospel that we are transformed. Even if you have raised a moral child, it is possible you have not raised a godly child.

4. Dean, *Almost Christian*, 18.

It is a foolish father who thinks he alone can teach his children all they need to know. So if he is serious about transferring the Christian faith to his children, he will work in close partnership with his wife, and together, they will see to it that their children are in church on Sundays, being cared for and taught by other adults who reinforce at church what they are learning at home. They will not make their children's busy extracurricular schedules the center of family life. Instead, they will require their children to attend church with them just as they require their children to attend school, and they will pray that their children will grow to love it. By making public worship of God on the Lord's Day a priority, they will teach them that God is more important than club soccer and baseball travel teams. They will do this even though this sport-worshiping culture conspires against them. They will do this because they are Christian parents.

As Christian parents, we form alliances with one another in helping to raise each other's children in the covenant community of faith. I treasure the investment that so many adults in my church made in our children. As my son grew up, I took him with me on camping trips, hunting trips, fishing trips, and mission trips along with my friends. He observed first-hand how Christian men talk and act and think and laugh and joke and pray and treat each other. To this day, though he is now married and moved away, he knows that my friends at this church are his "uncles in the Lord" who will do anything they can for his good. In addition, my children grew up under the sound teaching and creative outreach of strong youth pastors who love teenagers. I largely attribute any parenting success we have had to those men and women in our church who taught and cared for our children. Sadly, those teenagers whose parents are not personally devoted to teaching and applying Scripture at home and who do not make active, significant involvement in church life a priority do not usually thrive as Christians on the college campus or in emerging adulthood.

Where Are the Men?

So we pray that our children grow up and seek out believing spouses, establishing Christian homes that bear testimony to the world of God's love and grace. Yet for many young single women in the church, this is a huge challenge. Where are the men? Mark Regnerus writes that "the ratio of devoutly Christian young women to men is far from even. Among evangelical churchgoers, there are about three single women for every two single men." In most churches, even in conservative evangelical churches, there is a "shortage of young Christian men."[5]

There are more women in most churches than men, and often the men who are in church don't know as much as the women about the Bible. Add to this, there is more fatherlessness than motherlessness. About 30 percent of children in America currently live in a single parent home, and 80 percent of those homes are headed by mothers. Half of all children in America will live in a single parent home at some time before they turn 18. Children raised in single parent, fatherless homes are more likely to be in poverty, go to prison, get pregnant out of wedlock, have an abortion, struggle in school, experience depression, and attempt suicide. They are also less likely to attend church.[6] Not surprisingly, teenagers who are "highly devoted" to the Christian faith "tend to have highly devoted parents who are married and well-educated."[7]

There are, of course, many single mothers in our churches who are heroically leading their children to follow Christ. I am grateful for these women in our own church and I am encouraged by their faithfulness. They lay down their lives for their children, paying the price in secret sacrifices that none but God can see. Yet they are not raising their children alone. Our church family surrounds and supports them, giving their children models of Christian manhood. The success that many of these single moms experience in raising godly kids does not suggest we need fewer godly men in the church, but instead makes the case we need more of them.

So the church needs credible men. George Gallup notes that "women may be the backbone of a congregation, but the presence of a significant number of men is often a clear indicator of spiritual health."[8] God designed men to lead at home and in the church. "Fathers," exhorts the apostle Paul, "do not provoke your children to anger, but bring them up in the discipline and instruction of the Lord" (Eph 6:4). Certainly, mothers should be teaching their children the ways of the Lord, but Christ-loving mothers desire to

5. Regnerus, "The Case for Early Marriage."

6. Waite and Gallagher, *Case for Marriage*, 129.

7. Dean, *Almost Christian*, 47.

8. Murrow, *Why Men Hate Going*, 37. In fact, if you are a man reading this book right now, you and I are beating the odds. Women buy about 75 percent of Christian books, and booksellers adjust their marketing appropriately. Men don't buy and read as many books as women. Of the top hundred Christian books, there are normally three times more books specifically directed to women than men. Not surprisingly, there are more women writing books than there are men (Murrow, 65–66).

be in partnership with a husband who assumes the role of a servant leader, neither pushy nor passive.

When it comes to biblical instruction that is "centered in the home," write J. I. Packer and Gary Parrett, "there can be no question that the Bible puts the burden of instruction primarily on parents, and especially on fathers."[9] David Murrow observes that "in spiritual matters kids tend to follow their fathers. Throughout human history, men have been the religious leaders of society. A Christianity without significant masculine presence will atrophy and die."[10]

I believe that there is a shortage of young Christian men because there is a shortage of old Christian men. There are too few seasoned and credible veterans of the Christian life who are capable of taking younger men under their spiritual wing and helping them get established in a life of following Christ. In the American church, there is a dangerous shortage of credible men.

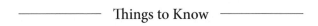

———————— Things to Know ————————

– What are the two greatest predictors of whether or not your children will hold to the Christian faith?

9. Packer and Parrett, *Grounded in the Gospel*, 195.
10. Murrow, *Why Men Hate Going*, 48.

$$—— 3 ——$$

A Credible Man

I think it's my faith that keeps me grounded, especially because I'm a Christ-fol-lower for sure. Live like Christ and He'll live in you. And that's what I want to do.

—MILEY CYRUS AT THE AGE OF 15[1]

. . . the pastors of the churches act most wisely when they early and carefully catechize the youth, laying the first grounds of faith, and faithfully teaching the rudiments of our religion by expounding the Ten Commandments, the Apostles' Creed, the Lord's Prayer and the doctrines of the sacraments, with other such principles and chief heads of our religion.

—THE SECOND HELVETIC CONFESSION, 1566[2]

"THERE ARE TWO THINGS you can do on earth, but you can't do in heaven." That's what the speaker said and immediately, he had my attention. I don't remember the details of his message, but I remember this clear statement.[3] What are the two things?

First, you can't sin in heaven. In heaven, the believer who daily fought temptation, daily failed, and daily asked for God's forgiveness will fight no more. In that glorified state, the war with sin will finally be over.

Second, you can't tell unbelievers about Jesus in heaven. There will be no unbelievers in heaven and everyone there already knows Jesus.

Okay. That makes sense.

But then he asked a question.

---

1. McKay, "Pop Tarts."

2. 25:1.

3. The speaker was Rick Warren, Senior Pastor of Saddleback Church in Lake Forest, California.

"Of those two things, which one did God leave you here on earth to do? Why didn't he just take you to heaven the moment you trusted Christ as your savior? Did he leave you here so you could sin some more? No! The reason you are here is to glorify God by telling the world about Jesus."

Okay. That makes sense too.

Every Christian Man's Duty

Every Christian man has the privilege and responsibility to bear witness to Jesus Christ (Acts 1:8). As Jesus sent out his apostles to be witnesses of what they saw (the death of Christ for our sins, his burial, and his resurrection), all Christians are authorized to bear witness to the apostles' message and how they have come to believe it (Acts 2:42; 2 Tim 2:2; 1 Pet 3:15). For Christian men, bearing witness begins at home, offering a credible testimony to our wives and children. It doesn't end there, for we are also commanded to make "disciples of all nations" (Matt 28:19–20), so we bear witness to our friends, neighbors, and co-workers. This is how we fight this war. Not by violent force, but by persuasive words, speaking the truth in love, urging people to come to Christ. But men, when you open your mouth to speak, why should anyone listen to you? What makes you a credible witness for Christ?

The first obstacle to getting a fair hearing is _ignorance_. If you don't know what you are talking about, you will soon be found out. If you don't get your facts straight when it comes to the Bible, people will summarily dismiss your testimony. If you cannot articulate and defend the Christian faith, don't expect your children to go much beyond your level of competency. If you are biblically illiterate, you are entering the battle unarmed. You cannot pass on what you do not possess.

The second obstacle is _hypocrisy_. It is hard to determine which man does more damage to the cause of Christ: a man who doesn't know what he's talking about or a man who knows but doesn't _do_ what he's talking about. Even if you can ably present Christian doctrine and skillfully make the case for it, the impact of your words is diminished if you do not live in submission to that doctrine. If you are angry, arrogant, or selective in the commands of Scripture you choose to obey, your testimony is damaged goods. Even people who don't go to church know that we should practice what we preach. So,

Ignorance + Hypocrisy = No Credibility

When it comes to transferring the faith to the next generation, many men are disqualified because they lack credibility. Credibility comprises two main components that remove the two obstacles. The first component is *competence*. A competent man can articulate and defend his faith in Jesus Christ. He will be able to explain the core doctrines of Christianity to his own children as well as his friends. Though unbelievers may not agree with him, they will conclude that he is an able spokesman for the Christian faith.

The second component is *character*. A man of character proves over time to be humble, disciplined, kind, and trustworthy. He not only knows the Bible, but earnestly labors to obey it. When hypocrisy corrupts a man's life, his wife finds it difficult to respect him. When our children see a duplicitous lifestyle in us, acting one way at church and another at home, they want less to do with our religion. Unbelievers leverage our hypocrisy as one more excuse to summarily dismiss the claims of Christ. What they all need to see in us is character. To be a man of character is to be above reproach, a person of integrity, who speaks the truth, keeps his promises, and seeks to meet the real needs of others. Over the course of years, the Christian man patiently builds a good reputation, even with people outside of the church. He is not a perfect man, but when he errs, he takes responsibility, repents, and makes it right.

The Most Credible Man

Let's keep it simple. If you don't remember anything else, remember that your goal is to become more like Jesus. When you read about the fruit of the Spirit in Galatians 5:22–23 for example, note that it is simply a catalogue of the virtues of Jesus. During his earthly ministry, he perfectly manifested love, joy, peace, patience, kindness, goodness, faithfulness, gentleness, and self-control. Or think of the qualifications for an overseer in 1 Timothy 3:1– 7. As the Overseer of overseers, Jesus was and is a man "above reproach." Jesus showed us what it is like for a man to have character.

What about his competence? He was never bested in a debate. Never. His mastery of Scripture was evident to all and they were "astonished at his teaching" (Matt 7:28). Those who foolishly tried to trip him up were put to silence (Matt 22:34). Those who attempted to trap him in some logical inconsistency learned their lesson and did not "dare to ask him any more questions" (Matt 22:46). Jesus showed us what it is like for a man to have competence.

Working together, his peerless competence and perfect character gave him ultimate credibility.

Both/And

While competence is the ability to recall the *content* of the Bible, character is the humility that obeys the *commands* of the Bible. While competence is what you know, character is who you are, and it takes both elements to be a credible witness. It is possible to be competent, a good debater, and yet lack character. It is also possible to be a man of character, a good man, but lack competence in articulating and defending the faith. A credible man is the one with both character and competence securely in place and growing.

Think about it. When you hire a new employee, do you want someone with competence or character? When your alma mater searches for a new head coach, do you hope they find someone who has competence (he can recruit and win) or one who has character (he will protect your school from NCAA sanctions)? If you are a marketing executive selling golf equipment, do you want to secure an endorser who has competence (he can win on the tour) or character (he is faithful to his super-model wife)?

The answer of course is that you want and even demand both. We demand both in our surgeons, our pilots, and the young men who want to marry our daughters. It is not *either/or* but *both/and*. Why should it be any different when it comes to bearing witness for Christ? What kind of man will God use to bring him the most glory: men with competence or character? God always has, and always will, use men with both. His design is to use a credible man. So,

Competence + Character = Credibility

God only knows how many young Americans abandoned the church because they knew a church member who lacked credibility. Sadly, nearly three out of four unchurched people believe "the church is full of hypocrites."[4] Drew Dyck surmises that most young people who leave the church "have been exposed to a superficial form of Christianity that effectively inoculated them against authentic faith."[5]

In our attempts to be culturally relevant, we have too often dumbed down the faith, underestimating the ability of our children to learn the

4. Kelly, "Study: Unchurched Americans."
5. Dyck, *Generation Ex-Christian*, 43.

vocabulary of historic Christianity. As Susan Hunt writes, "When a child is born into our family, we do not revert to cooing and babbling in order to be baby-friendly . . . I intentionally use words I want the children to learn."[6] Instead of teaching solid, sturdy doctrine, the church gave our children motivational messages designed to elevate their self-esteem. Instead of giving them authentic role models who denied themselves, took up the cross, and followed Jesus, the church gave them babysitters who entertained them with silly games and slick presentations. We didn't challenge them to learn sound doctrine or think critically and they easily met our low expectations. To make matters worse, many significant men in their lives who professed to be Christians did not prove to be credible witnesses. Consequently, when we send many of our kids to the university, we are not sending troops to the battle but lambs to the slaughter.

A Modest and Ancient Proposal

I am optimistic that we can stop the bleeding, but it will not be easy. Neither will it be novel. It is not simply a matter of more programs, trendy techniques, or innovative approaches. There is nothing new in what I am proposing. In fact, it is mostly very old. My thesis is this: the church is healthiest when large numbers of adults, especially men, are actively involved in the time-tested process of catechizing.

Catechism is from a Greek word that means "to instruct orally," "to make hear," or "to echo back" and for centuries that's what men did. They orally instructed their children and new believers who came into the church. They made them hear the Ten Commandments, the Lord's Prayer, and the Apostles' Creed. They asked them questions about the core doctrines of the Christian faith and expected them to echo back the answers. They did not necessarily do this in a classroom setting but also at the dinner table, walking down the road, or riding on a horse.

This was not a mere transfer of information. An essential part of catechizing is modeling the life that is being taught, not just telling, but showing. The teacher must be trustworthy, sincerely devoted to Christ, genuinely interested in his students, creating an environment where the student feels safe enough to ask tough questions and even express real doubt without fear of condemnation.

6. Hunt, *Heirs of the Covenant*, 46.

Christians have done this before. In the historic creeds, confessions, and catechisms of the church, we find the heart of the Christian faith as it has been passed down through the generations. So in this book, I will refer to documents that are centuries old. To remind us that we are not breaking new ground, that we stand on the shoulders of giants, and that we are not the first generation of parents to face this dilemma, the second opening quote of every chapter of this book will be from one of these documents. Some of the wording is archaic and may be difficult for you at first, but your labor will be rewarded.

What Children Need Their Dads to Know

There will be thousands of unplanned teachable moments with your children. The Lord will give you ample opportunity to arm your sons and daughters with the Word, but will you see the opportunities for what they are and will you be ready when they come? While it is never too late to get started, I can tell you from personal experience and every study I've seen on the subject, the sooner you start the better. The foundation of your parenting work should be done by the time your son or daughter is fourteen.[7] Start the day you bring your son home from the hospital and use every opportunity you can to teach him. Be alert on football fields and baseball diamonds, in fishing boats and duck blinds. Be diligent while helping your daughter with her homework, driving her to soccer practice, washing the dog, or tinkering in the garage. Intentionally look for any opening for catechizing your kids. If you do this right, they will learn, but they often won't even know that you're teaching them. They are watching and listening more than you know in these years.

What Wives Need Their Husbands to Know

The purpose of this book is to help men become more credible witnesses for Christ in their homes, in their churches, at work, and in their communities. The scope is limited to seven basic things that every Christian man ought to know. Our wives need us to know these things. Some of our wives may not know that yet. They might not say that these are things they *want*

7. Smith, *Souls in Transition*, 247. "The vast majority, then, of those youth—85 percent—who have by the age of 18–23 ever committed to live their lives for God appear to have made their first commitments before the age of 14."

you to know, but these are certainly things they *need* you to know, and the sooner you know them, the better. Likewise, our children, our churches, our neighbors, and our nation need us to know these things, practice these things, defend these things, and invest them in the next generation.

The situation is urgent but there is hope. In the Bible and throughout church history, we have seen these defections before. We have seen God's people waver, retreat, and lose ground in one generation, only to see God come to the rescue in the next. God has never given up on his people and he will not give up on us now. By his grace, we can repent. We can return. We can reform. We can rebuild what has been torn down. And it begins, I believe, by recovering seven things that many professing Christians have forgotten, if they ever knew them. These seven things form the essential core of historic, apostolic Christianity. These are seven things that every Christian man should know and pass down to the next generation. These are seven things worth fighting for.

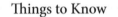 Things to Know

- What are 2 obstacles to credibility?
- What are 2 components of credibility?

4

Eighteen Years Is Shorter Than You Think

Me and my family got out of that [Christianity] and came to LA. To see all
forms of meditation and prayer made me less judgmental.

−JESSICA SIMPSON, SINGER AND ACTRESS[1]

Question 1: What is the chief end of man?

Answer. Man's chief end is to glorify God, and to enjoy him forever.

−WESTMINSTER SHORTER CATECHISM, 1648

I WAS CONCERNED FOR my wife. We had just moved our son into his dorm
for his freshman year of college. Our firstborn was leaving the nest, and so
much of my wife's life was invested in his. I was certain Lori would crack
when we gave him that last hug, but she held surprisingly steady. I'll never
forget the sight of Josh in my rear view mirror, standing alone, watching
us drive away. And then something happened I didn't expect. I began to
cry for the first time in a long time. My wife put her hand on my shoulder,
comforting me and reminding me we might actually see our son again. He
might even come home for a visit at Thanksgiving. It wasn't like he was
going to war. Right?

Long before that day, I had raced motorcycles, and it didn't take long
for Josh to take to the sport. Much of our time together revolved around
competing in the mud and blood, replacing piston rings, using WD-40 by
the gallon, and visiting our local orthopedic surgeon. Josh soon surpassed
me, learning to do things with a motocross bike I had only dreamed of. Unfortunately for me, the route home from his college campus that day took
us past three of the motocross tracks where he regularly competed and we

1. WENN, "Simpson Shies Away."

had spent a lot of father-son time. As we passed each track, the memories flooded back and the tears returned.

What was happening to me? In times like these, a lot of things go through a father's mind. Where did the time go? Did I do my job? Did I give him a good example? Did I teach him everything he will need to be successful?

And what does it mean to be successful? That's a question that every Christian man needs to settle, for his own sake and the sake of his family. Christians have pondered this question for centuries and church leaders have made it a focal point of their instruction. One of the most famous treatments is found in the first question of the Westminster Catechism:

> *What is the chief end of man?*

Other ways to ask the question: What is your purpose in life? Why were you created? Why do you exist? How will you know if you spent your life well or squandered it? To ask it from a parenting angle: What is the purpose of your child's life? Why does your son exist? How will your daughter know if she has spent her life well or wasted it?

Gravitas and Purpose

The answer found in the Westminster Catechism is pointed and pregnant with meaning:

> Man's chief end is to glorify God, and to enjoy him forever.

What does it mean to glorify God? Centuries ago, Thomas Watson observed that when we speak of the glory of God, there is a "two-fold" glory, two senses in which "the glory of God" is understood.[2] The first is God's intrinsic glory that he has in himself. It is so essential to his character that God cannot be God without it. Therefore, he will not part with it and declares, "My glory I will not give to another" (Isa 48:11). The second sense is the glory we ascribe to God. "Ascribe to the Lord the glory due his name" (1 Chr 16:29). To ascribe glory is to attribute glory to God, to freely and gladly admit to ourselves and all others that God is intrinsically glorious. It is only right for Christians to glorify God since he *created* us. He is the Creator and we are the creatures. Furthermore, it is only right for Christians to glorify God since he *redeemed* us. "You were bought with a price. So glorify God

---

2. Watson, *Body of Divinity*, 11.

in your body" (1 Cor 6:20). We give him glory because he is our Creator and Redeemer. These are the two senses in which the Bible speaks of God's glory: intrinsic and ascribed.

In the Old Testament, *glory* most often translates the Hebrew word, *kavod*, which literally means "heavy" or "weighty." It can be used to describe someone of great importance and moral authority. For example, a king may be "heavy" with knowledge and wisdom, silver and gold, or soldiers and swords. The term in Latin is *gravitas*, which is often used today to describe someone who is clearly deserving of honor and respect. To say a man has *gravitas* is to say he is not to be taken lightly. Rather he is a man to be respected and reckoned with. In his presence, it is best not to speak until you are spoken to.

But even the best and most dignified men fall short. The *gravitas* of earthly presidents and prime ministers, popes and pastors, or surgeons and scientists pales in comparison to the *gravitas* of God. "The Lord is high above all nations, and his glory above the heavens!" (Ps 113:4). God is not like us. He has *gravitas* we cannot imagine. Even the smartest, strongest, and best among us are less than intellectual, physical, and moral featherweights compared to God. Therefore, glorifying God requires us to know and make known his *gravitas*, his weightiness, his utmost importance, his moral perfection, his infinite wisdom, his limitless wealth, his matchless love, his sovereign power, and his ultimate authority.

In the New Testament, *kavod* is usually translated in the Greek as *doxa*, which originally meant "opinion" or "judgment" but is used by New Testament authors to describe the high opinion and good judgment that we owe to someone who is worthy of it. Since God is perfect in all of his attributes, to glorify him is to give him the praise he deserves. Simply put, *to glorify God means to think, say, and do the things that direct the world's attention to the only true and living God.*

First Corinthians 10:31 serves as the main proof text for the framers of the Westminster Catechism's first question: "So, whether you eat or drink, or whatever you do, do all to the glory of God." Paul has just rebuked the Corinthian church for allowing its members to attend the feasts of idol worship without regard for their own weakness in resisting temptation or the weakness of others. By foolishly placing themselves in dangerous circumstances, surrounded by pagan worship and sexual sin, many of them easily fell into immorality. Not only that, by their example they led other Christians into immorality.

The result was that Christians lost credibility, the church was divided, evangelism was displaced, and the advance of the gospel was halted. Instead of *directing* the attention of their family, friends, and neighbors from idols to the true God, their words and actions were *distracting* attention from the true God to false idols. Instead of leading others to worship "the Creator, who is blessed forever" (Rom 1:25), they led them to worship the creation. Paul admonishes them to consider that even the briefest conversations and the smallest actions can direct the world's attention either *to* God or *from* God. Therefore, "*whatever* you do, do all to the glory of God." Whatever you do will either *direct* people to God or *distract* people from him.

To glorify God is to shine a spotlight on him and say to the world, "Look! Stop what you are doing and look! Here is our God and Maker. Just look at his magnificence! See who he is, note what he has done, and listen to what he has said. He alone is worthy of all praise, honor, and thanks. And he alone is your hope and help. He alone has all you need. He is at the center of all things and he must not be ignored." Through Isaiah, God declares that this is the purpose of his chosen people, "whom I created for my glory" (Isa 43:7).

In the New Testament, the glory of God is associated with Jesus. Because "the glory of the Lord shone around them" at the announcement of Christ's birth, the shepherds outside Bethlehem were "filled with great fear" (Luke 2:9). John could write that "the Word became flesh, and dwelt among us, and we have seen his glory" (John 1:14). The writer of Hebrews assures his readers that Jesus "is the radiance of the glory of God" (Heb 1:1–3). To glorify Jesus is to glorify God since he and the Father are one (John 10:30). To say it another way, it is impossible to properly glorify God apart from glorifying Jesus. Conversely, to dishonor Jesus, as most of the world does, is to dishonor God.

How do we glorify God?

When we glorify God, we are not adding anything to God's intrinsic glory. He is perfectly and infinitely glorious in himself and we have no glory to give him of our own. God is not "served by human hands, as though he needed anything" (Acts 17:25). Rather we glorify God by declaring, showing, displaying, or manifesting his glory. We do this by praising him for who he is and what he has done (Ps 96:8), by giving him thanks and acknowledging that all of our good comes from him (1 Tim 4:4), by confessing our sin instead of trying to hide it (Josh 7:19), by trusting him to keep his promises (Rom 4:20), by obeying his commands (John 17:4), by being faithful to him even in suffering (1 Pet 1:7), by giving money to his church (2 Cor 9:13), by doing good works (Matt 5:16), by living honorable lives (1 Pet 2:12), by rejoicing in the salvation of others (Acts 11:18), by advancing the spread of the gospel, sending missionaries, and bringing others to Christ. "By this," said Jesus, "is my Father glorified, that you bear much fruit and so prove to be my disciples" (John 15:8).

We can and should glorify God even in the most common everyday things. Go to work for the glory of God, attend class for the glory of God, pay your bills for the glory of God, do your customers right for the glory of God, feast for the glory of God, fast for the glory of God, take a nap for the glory of God, make love to your wife for the glory of God, abstain from sex for the glory of God, take your son fishing for the glory of God, take your daughter to dinner for the glory of God, learn to speak Spanish for the glory of God, exercise for the glory of God, mow your lawn for the glory of God, sharpen your short game for the glory of God, read a book for the glory of God, write a book for the glory of God, be a preacher, a plumber, or a pulmonary surgeon for the glory of God, live for the glory of God, and die for the glory of God (John 21:18). No matter where you are, what time it is, or who you are with, "whatever you do, do all to the glory of God" (1 Cor 10:31).

The man who glorifies God will stand out as unique and uncommon. Some men will hate him in the same way men hated Christ (John 15:18) while other men will conclude, "If that's what Jesus does to a man, I want to find out more about Jesus." You will either be reviled or respected, but either way, when you glorify God, your life will make a difference.

---------------- Things to Know ----------------

- What are the 2 senses in which the Bible speaks of the "glory of God?"

—— 5 ——

The Mission of a Christian Man

I'm not Buddhist, I'm not Hindu, I'm not Christian, but I still feel like I have a
deep connection with God.

−KATY PERRY, SINGER[1]

Touching the Lord Jesus, of whom Moses and the Prophets wrote, and whom the
Apostles preached, is the Son of God the Father, the brightness of his glory ...

−[FIRST] LONDON CONFESSION, 1644[2]

Do you have a mission statement for your life? Chances are good that
your company has a mission statement. So do your company's competitors.
So do your customers and clients. Your church may even have a mission
statement. But what about you? Do you have a personal mission statement?
What in the world are you doing? Are you clear about your life objectives?
How will you know if you spent your life well or wasted it?

Four Ways to Glorify God

As we saw in the last chapter, our mission is to glorify God. It's crucial to
recognize that glorifying God is inextricably linked to Jesus who is "the
Lord of glory" (1 Cor 2:8). There are at least four ways we glorify God in
our relationship with Jesus.

First, we glorify God by knowing Jesus. We begin knowing Jesus when
we hear the gospel and receive him as our Savior (John 1:12), trusting in
his work on the cross for our salvation. At this point we enter into a new

1 Hoffman, "Katy Conquers All."

2. Section 9.

relationship with him that lasts for all eternity. God adopts us into his family and Jesus becomes our Lord, our eldest brother (Heb 2:17; Rom 8:17), and our best friend (Matt 11:19; John 15:13). We will spend the rest of our lives on earth and in eternity getting to know him better.

Knowing Jesus at least means we know *about* him. That is, we gather as many facts as we can that help us understand who he is and what he is like. We do this in all of our relationships. When two people fall in love, they naturally want to find out about each other as each becomes a student of the other, learning more each day. Likewise we become students of Jesus, finding out what he cares about, what pleases him, what he loves, what he hates, what he said, what he did, what he is doing now, and what his plans are for the future, especially how those plans include us.

Knowing Jesus requires you to do theology (the study of God). You will spend the rest of your life gathering, systematizing, and harmonizing this information and just when you think you have Jesus somewhat figured out, he will surprise you. You will find something in the Bible you had not seen before, and it will take you to a deeper level of understanding. And as you grow in your knowledge of him, you will find that it is worth making great sacrifices to know him even better, learning to say with Paul, "I count everything as loss because of the surpassing worth of knowing Christ Jesus my Lord" and you will shamelessly declare to the world "I want to know him" (Phil 3:8,10).

Second, we glorify God by loving Jesus. To know Jesus is to love him. To love him is to hold him as dear and precious to us. Satan knows a lot *about* Jesus but does not love him because he doesn't *know* Jesus. If you know Jesus, really know him, you will love him. You will cherish him above all others. You will be so impressed with who he is and what he has done that you will be drawn to him and set your affections on him. In fact, loving Jesus is one of the marks of being a true child of God. "If God were your Father," said Jesus, "you would love me" (John 8:42).

Third, we glorify God by obeying Jesus. Obedience to Jesus is the inevitable fruit of loving him. "If you love me," Jesus said, "you will keep my commandments" (John 14:15) and "whoever has my commandments and keeps them, he it is who loves me" (John 14:21). John reinforces the truth: "By this we know that we have come to know him, if we keep his commandments. Whoever says 'I know him' but does not keep his commandments is a liar" (1 John 2:3–4). Profoundly, Jesus himself leads the way in showing how obedience glorifies God. At the end of his life, he could pray, "I have glorified you on earth having accomplished the work you gave me to do" (John 17:4). Likewise, we glorify God when we obey him and accomplish the work he gives us to do.

If we obey Jesus, we will love God with all of our hearts and love our neighbors as we love ourselves as he commanded (Matt 22:37–38). In doing good to our neighbors, Christians point our neighbors to Christ, and by pointing them to Christ, we point them to God. That's why Jesus said to his disciples that people will see their "good works and give glory to your Father who is in heaven" (Matt 5:16).

Fourth, we glorify God by exalting Jesus. Because "Jesus Christ is Lord, to the glory of God the Father" (Phil 2:11), he is to be exalted, lifted up, so all can see him. He should be the center of attention in all things. There are two ways to exalt the Lord Jesus. The first way is in our evangelism (proclaiming the gospel). Here we exalt Jesus by telling people how great God is and by sending missionaries to the gospel-deprived places on this planet to tell people how great God is. We are to praise the Lord "among the nations" (Ps 18:49) and "declare his glory among the nations" (Ps 96:3) so they might come to know, love, obey, and exalt Jesus (Matt 28:18–20). This missionary endeavor will be successful because God is committed to it. Ultimately, the Lord Jesus "will be exalted among the nations" (Ps 46:10).

Another way we exalt the Lord is in our worship, telling *God* how great he is. We are to "magnify the Lord" and "exalt his name" with other Christians (Ps 34:3). "Exalt the Lord," commands the psalmist, "worship at his footstool" (Ps 99:5). Our public worship should include "singing and making melody to the Lord" (Eph 3:16). We "sing praises to him" and "tell of all of his wondrous works" (1 Chr 16:9) not because he needs to hear them but because we need to hear ourselves and each other singing and saying them. So we exalt Christ by telling other people (evangelism) and God himself (worship) how great he is.

Taken altogether, I think that this is what the Westminster Catechism means when it says we are to enjoy God. We will find incomparable and enduring joy in knowing, loving, obeying, and exalting Jesus Christ. This is how we obey the command to delight ourselves in the Lord (Ps 37:4). Real joy comes when we can say to the Lord there is "nothing on earth I desire besides you" (Ps 73:25). We will be fully satisfied and happy in him. While the rest of the world seeks to be satisfied in the creation, true contentment is found only in the Creator. "Our hearts are restless," confessed Augustine of Hippo, "until they rest in you."[3]

Unbelievers frantically seek happiness in possessions, positions, people, pleasure, and power only to find they have believed a lie. After obtaining these things, there remains a hollowness in their hearts, an enduring emptiness. Blaise Pascal, the seventeenth-century mathematician and philosopher, noted that emptiness (which some of Pascal's readers have referred to as a "God-shaped vacuum") which man "in vain tries to fill from all his surroundings, seeking from things absent the help he does not obtain in things present. But these are all inadequate because the infinite abyss can only be filled by an infinite and immutable object, that is to say, only by God himself."[4] Idols never satisfy.

This has massive implications for your life. You glorify God not only by knowing, loving, obeying, and exalting Jesus. *Your mission is to glorify God by helping people know, love, obey, and exalt Jesus Christ.* How's that for a mission statement?

That The Next Generation Might Know Them

Knowing your mission helps you know your job description as a man. As a single man, you follow the lead of Jesus and Paul, both single men, to make disciples. As a husband and father, you lead your wife and children to God, using every God-given resource to help them move God up higher in their opinions so that they in turn will glorify him. As a friend, colleague, competitor, employee, or boss, with your lips and your life, you call attention to God in your sphere of influence. And your mission starts at home.

This is why fathers are implored to teach the Word of God "diligently to your children" (Deut 6:7; 11:19), using every opportunity and available means to invest God's Word in their heart. That's why the psalmist says, "We will not hide them from their children, but tell to the coming generation the glorious deeds of the Lord and his might and the wonders that he has done" (Ps 78:4). Why did God command fathers to teach God's laws to their kids? So *"that the next generation might know them,* the children yet unborn, and arise and tell them to their children" (Ps 78:5–6, italics mine). Each generation is responsible to make sure the next generation is familiar with the stellar record of God's faithfulness "so that a people yet to be created may praise the

3. Augustine, *Confessions, and Enchiridion,* Book 1, Chapter 1.

4. Pascal, *Pensees,* #425.

Lord" (Ps 102:18). For the glory of God, fathers are to bring up their children "in the discipline and instruction of the Lord" (Eph 6:4).

The Five A's of Success

This chapter is choked with quotes from the Bible for a reason. I want to demonstrate the point Jonathan Edwards made over two hundred and fifty years ago when he said it "appears that all that is ever spoken of in the Scripture as an ultimate end of God's works is included in that one phrase, 'the glory of God.'"[5] Likewise, over five hundred years ago, John Calvin declared that "there is no part of our life, and no action so minute, that it ought not to be directed to the glory of God."[6]

Across every culture, success is measured by achievement in five areas. The world rewards accomplishments in these five areas with riches and recognition. *Academics* has to do with intelligence and education and is often measured by GPAs. *Athletics* has to do with the physical strength, speed, and dexterity that are displayed in sports and measured in statistics like ERAs, rushing yards, and a bench press max. *Arts* has to do with the ability to create objects of beauty or to perform on stage by singing, playing an instrument, dancing, entertaining, or acting. *Appearance* has to do with physical attractiveness, striking facial structure, beautiful bodies, hairstyles, and clothes. *Affluence* is the result of using success in the other four areas as a commodity. The world will pay good money to add a brilliant computer programmer to the staff, watch a big-leaguer turn a double play, listen to the latest American idol, or gaze on a flawless (and digitally enhanced) face on a magazine cover. Affluence is marked by status symbols and draws the praise and envy of all people.

In themselves, these things are not evil and teaching our children how to excel in them is part of a father's job. But the question is this: Why? Why excel? Why achieve? Why succeed? Our children will be constantly, cleverly, and viciously tempted to excel in these things for their own glory. At times, they will swell with pride, and actually believe the adoring words that people will say about them. At times they will think they are at the center of the universe, and they will be frustrated when the rest of us don't acknowledge that. They will often plunge into despair when others criticize them or they realize they cannot even trust in themselves, for they do not

5. Edwards, *Works*, 1:119.
6. Calvin, *Commentaries*, 20:347.

make good gods. They will air their own press releases, desperately seeking the approval of their audience. They will find clever ways to brag and boast and bring attention to their achievements. Like Herod, who "did not give God the glory" (Acts 12:23), they will try to take credit for things God has done in, for, and through them. In short, they will try to rob God of his glory. Our job will be to teach them to say, "Not to us, O Lord, not to us, but to your name give glory" (Ps 115:1).

There is a way to make the Dean's list and dunk a basketball for God's glory. There is a way to paint portraits, design buildings, and sing songs for God's glory. There is a way to stay fit, dress well, and style your hair for God's glory. There is a way to turn a profit, achieve excellence, and be successful for God's glory. Raising children for God's glory does not mean we try to produce underachievers.

After writing new music, the famed composer Johann Sebastian Bach had a custom of writing the letters "SDG" at the bottom of the manuscript. In this cryptic reference to the Latin phrase *Soli Deo Gloria*, which means "Glory to God alone," Bach was careful to give credit where credit was due. The fact that we still talk about it today is a tribute to his success in glorifying God. Likewise, if God chooses to entrust talent and treasure to your children, helping them achieve excellence, there is great potential for them to deflect the praise and adoration they receive from the world to its rightful place at the feet of Jesus, but it will not happen naturally. They need to be taught. They must be catechized. That's your job. If your daughter enters her freshman year of college with an academic scholarship but biblically illiterate, something got off track. If by the age of 18 your son can field a short-hop ground ball but cannot field the most basic questions about the Christian faith, it is possible that you have not done your job.

——————— Things to Know ———————

- What are 4 ways we glorify God in our relationship with Jesus?

$$—\ 6\ —$$

A Big, Strange, Wonderful, Difficult Book

If the Bible was written by God, why is stuff in the Bible untrue?

−BILL MAHR, COMEDIAN AND TELEVISION HOST[1]

All things in Scripture are not alike plain in themselves, nor alike clear unto all; yet those things which are necessary to be known, believed and observed for salvation, are so clearly propounded and opened in some place of Scripture or other, that not only the learned, but the unlearned, in a due use of ordinary means, may attain to a sufficient understanding of them.

−WESTMINSTER CONFESSION OF FAITH, 1647[2]

THE STORY IS THE stuff of legends. The Green Bay Packers had suffered multiple losing seasons and morale was low. After losing ten of their twelve games the previous year, the Packers hired Vince Lombardi in 1959 as the head coach and charged him with the task of turning things around. He didn't see the progress that first year he had hoped for and he knew the key to success was focusing on the fundamentals. At one frustrating point in the training camp of 1961, he gathered the team, held up an oblong mass of inflated leather and said, "Gentlemen, this is a football." To which one of the players replied, "Uh, Coach, could you slow down a little. You're going too fast for us."[3]

I can't assume anything about the average Christian's basic knowledge of the Bible. Maybe some of you will read this chapter and think, "Of course! I knew that. Who doesn't know that?" Answer: Most Christians. Most Christians no longer know what Christians used to know. In generations

---

1 Clabough, "Bill Mahr Lashes Out."

2. 1:7.

3 Maraniss, *When Pride Still Mattered*, 274.

past, Christians were expected to know the books of the Bible. Go ahead. I dare you. Ask a friend of yours at church this Sunday if he can recite all sixty-six books of the canon in order. Ask him what a canon is. Why would your children think the Bible is important to you if you don't even know these most basic things? It's time to start at the beginning.

Men, this is a Bible.

The Bible is a Book

The English word "Bible" comes from the Greek word *biblion*, which means "book." The Bible is a book that answers our most important questions and addresses our greatest needs. What we need most is to know God, but all we know about God is what he chooses to reveal, and God reveals himself in two ways. In *general revelation*, he reveals himself to all human beings through creation. No matter where you live, you can study the stars, consider the complexity of the human hand, feel the tug of your conscience, or decipher the code of DNA and reach the conclusion that God exists. The existence of creation argues for the existence of a Creator, and we can reasonably infer from creation that the Creator is orderly, intelligent, and powerful.

Although we can learn some things through the creation, we cannot find all we need to know about God in the creation. General revelation is sufficient to show all people that God is there, that we owe him our obedience, and that we have broken his laws, but general revelation cannot lead us to a solution. For this reason, God reveals himself in special ways.

Special revelation builds on general revelation as God reveals himself directly to particular people. Through various means, God spoke to and through specific people so that "all Scripture is breathed out by God" (2 Tim 5:16–17). Historically, Christians have understood that the words of the Bible are the actual words of God. As the Westminster Confession puts it, the Bible is "Holy Scripture, or the Word of God written."[4]

So the Bible is a written record of the special revelation of God. It is, in effect, his autobiography, written over fourteen hundred years as he progressively revealed himself to the world. And like all autobiographies, it is selective. God doesn't tell us everything we may *want* to know about him, but he does tell us everything we *need* to know. When we read the Bible, or hear it read, and think carefully about what it says, we are listening to God.

4. Article 2.

Every Book Has a Structure

Open most books and you will find a table of contents. Good books have a structure, specifically designed by the author. There is a sense of progression as the author builds in each chapter on the foundation of the previous chapter. That's what you will find with the Bible. The revelation is progressive and takes place over many centuries. In the front of your Bible you will see a table of contents with sixty-six divisions. Each division represents one book, making the Bible a book of books.

The structure of the Bible has two main parts: The Old Testament has thirty-nine books and the New Testament twenty-seven books. Why are there just sixty-six books? There were other books written about God during the same period, so why weren't they included in the Bible? The short answer is that though there are many books written *about* God, only these 66 books are recognized by the church to be written *by* God.

The decision to include or exclude certain books was not arbitrary. Each book had to meet a strict criterion, called a *canon*. *Canon* is a Latin word which means "rule" or "standard." The canon is a list of all the books that meet certain standards and therefore should be in the Bible. What was the standard for Old Testament books? The short answer is that for Christians, Jesus' approval of these books is sufficient. By Jesus' day, the canon of the Old Testament, the Hebrew Scripture we call the Old Testament, was fixed. Jesus received this canon as the authoritative word of God and frequently quoted and explained it during his earthly ministry.

With regard to the New Testament, there are at least three tests. First, an apostle of Jesus Christ wrote the book. An apostle was an eyewitness of Jesus after his resurrection (Acts 1:22) and was directly authorized by Jesus to write Scripture. Twenty-two books of the New Testament meet this criterion. Second, if not written by an apostle, the book was written by someone who was directly supervised by an apostle. For example, Mark was an associate of the Apostle Peter and Luke served alongside the Apostle Paul. Paul recognizes the authority of Luke's writing (Luke and Acts), referring to it as scripture (1 Tim 5:18). Similarly, Peter recognizes Paul's letters as God-inspired scripture (2 Pet 3:16). So while the books of Mark, Luke, Acts, James, and Jude were not directly written by the original apostles, they meet this second standard of canonicity. Hebrews was probably admitted to the canon based on this criterion as well, even though there is considerable debate about its human author.

The third standard requires that all the books of the canon must be consistent with all other Scripture. For example, Romans cannot contradict Isaiah, and James cannot contradict Romans. These are three tests of the New Testament canon and we should not expect any more books to be included. The canon is now closed, since "long ago, at many times and in many ways, God spoke to our fathers by the prophets, but in these last days he has spoken to us by his Son" (Heb 1:1–2). Jesus and his apostles are the last word, and there is a sense of finality as we read in the last book of the Bible the sober warning that if anyone adds or takes away "from the words of this book of this prophecy, God will take away his share in the tree of life" (Rev 22:19).

Every Book Has an Author

Like every other book, the Bible has an author. Actually it has over forty human authors, from Moses to John. This adds to the uniqueness of the Bible, since these authors, often separated by centuries, wrote books that were completely compatible with one another. By now you may be confused, since a few pages ago I asserted that God wrote the Bible.

So who wrote the Bible? God or men? The answer is yes. Suppose you hire a general contractor to build a house. In turn, he hires a dozen sub-contractors who are responsible for different areas of construction. Soon the job site is swarming with excavators, framers, plumbers, roofers, and masons. So who built the house? The general contractor or the sub-contractors? The answer again is yes. The contractor worked through the subs and is ultimately responsible for the outcome. Similarly, God worked through over forty human authors and is ultimately responsible for the outcome. As the human authors of Scripture, these "men spoke from God as they were carried along by the Holy Spirit" (2 Pet 1:21).

Every Author Expects to Be Understood

I have a certain level of expectation of you, the reader of this book. I expect you to read my sentences carefully. I expect you to correctly connect subjects to verbs, and verbs to objects. I expect you to know when I'm exaggerating to make a point or using figurative language to drive that point home. I expect you to pick up on my sarcasm, define words the same way I do, and take the time to think through what I say. I expect you to balance my statements in this part of the book with statements I've made in other parts of the book. I expect you to know the definition of the word "expect." I think these are reasonable expectations.

God has similar expectations of us when we read his book. Like us, God does not want to be misunderstood and he hates to be misquoted. He warns us about spiritual leaders who "distort the word of God" (2 Cor 4:2) and church leaders who "distort the truth" (Acts 20:30). Some will be motivated by profit as "peddlers of God's word" (2 Cor 2:17). Whole churches "will not endure sound doctrine, but having itching ears they will accumulate for themselves teachers to suit their own passions" (2 Tim 4:3). Therefore, Christians should "contend for the faith that was once for all delivered to the saints" (Jude 3). If Christian men don't know the things they ought to know, history shows that they will be gullible, easily misled, pushed around, exploited, intimidated, and manipulated by the smooth talk of religious leaders who mishandle God's word.

"Do Unto Authors . . ."

To know God is to love God. And it is simply unloving to take someone's words out of context. It is unloving to twist those words to make them say something they were never intended to say. It is unloving to be lazy and distracted in our listening. It is unloving to ignore the time and setting in which those words were spoken or written. In the end, interpreting the Bible is all about obeying the Golden Rule. "So whatever you wish that others would do to you, do also to them" (Matt 7:12). Do you really want someone to misunderstand you? Put words in your mouth? Misquote you? Manipulate your statements to serve their personal agenda? Of course not. So why would we do that to God? In what John Piper calls "the golden rule of reading" you should "Do unto *authors* as you would have them do unto you."[5] Understanding the intent of the original author is the subject of the next chapter.

———————— Things to Know ————————

- What are the 2 kinds of revelation?
- What are the 66 books of the Bible?
- What are the 3 standards of the New Testament canon?

5. Piper, *Think*, 45.

— 7 —

Listening to the Texting God

I like the Bible. I'm just saying I don't like the way people misuse it . . . I like it as a book. Just like I like "The Cat in the Hat."

−MARILYN MANSON, AMERICAN ROCK MUSICIAN[1]

The infallible rule of interpretation of Scripture is the Scripture itself: and therefore, when there is a question about the true and full sense of any Scripture . . . it must be searched and known by other places that speak more clearly.

−WESTMINSTER CONFESSION OF FAITH, 1647[2]

MORE PEOPLE ON THIS planet own a cell-phone than a toothbrush[3] and about three fourths of them send texts rather than make calls.[4] Over six trillion text messages are sent every year, which is about 200,000 texts a second. The median number of texts sent by American teenagers alone is 60 a day.[5] Most of these texts are not models of syntax, grammar, spelling, or punctuation, but they get the job done if u no wat i mean lol. No doubt, a few thousand ambiguous and unclear texts are sent every second of every day that are not immediately coherent. The recipient opens the text message, reads it, and unconsciously engages in hermeneutics, the science of interpretation.

In a remarkable display of grace, God has texted us. The most important text message you will ever receive comes from your Creator. For that reason, no text deserves more careful scrutiny and disciplined hermeneutics than the Bible.

1. Manson, Interview by Bill Maher.
2. 1:9.
3. Hall, "Are There Really More."
4. Smith, "Americans and Text Messaging."
5. Lenhard, "Teens, Smartphones, and Texting."

There are seven basic rules of interpretation. There are certainly more than seven rules of interpretation, but these are a few essentials to get you started in reading and understanding the Bible. As you progress, you will add more rules that will guide you through the important process of listening to God in his Word. In general, these are the same rules you should apply when interpreting any written document, whether it is a text message, an email, a company memo, a song lyric, or the Constitution of the United States. God chose to speak to us in human language and all the conventional rules of human language apply.

1) Context Is King

A pair of Mormon missionaries found their way to my door one day with a Bible and a Book of Mormon in hand. In the course of our conversation, they presented their doctrine of the pre-existence of the human soul. Before we were born, they explained, we all existed in heaven, without bodies. At conception, God inserts that soul in a human body. "In our pre-earth life," they explained, "we lived in the presence of our heavenly Father as His spirit children. We did not have a physical body."[6] Fascinated, I asked them where the Bible supported this idea. They took me to Proverbs 8:25: "Before the mountains had been shaped, before the hills, I was brought forth."

I felt a mild panic as I read. Was the author of Proverbs claiming pre-existence? Suddenly, I remembered something that one of my college professors, Robertson McQuilkin, had taught me about interpreting the Bible: "Context is King."[7] One of the first steps to understanding any statement is to examine its immediate context. So I backed up the chapter to the verse where the speaker identifies herself: "I, wisdom, dwell together with prudence." With great relief, I realized that the poet of Proverbs was using a figure of speech called personification, attributing human characteristics to something non-human or abstract. In this case, wisdom is made to speak as a noble woman. When I pointed this out to my young guests, the conversation came to an abrupt end.

You cannot memorize everything in the Bible, but if you remember that "context is king," many of your questions will be answered. Examine the words that are "fore and aft" of the words you are trying to interpret. After you examine the immediate context of sentence, paragraph, and

6. Church of Jesus Christ of Latter Days Saints, "Pre-Earth Life."
7. McQuilkin, *Understanding and Applying the Bible*, 153.

chapter, expand your search to include the whole book, and eventually the whole Bible. In the end, the best commentary on the Bible is the Bible.

Probably the best single piece of advice you could ever get about interpreting the Bible comes from this line in the Westminster Confession of Faith:

> The infallible rule of interpretation of Scripture is the Scripture itself: and therefore, when there is a question about the true and full sense of any Scripture . . . it must be searched and known by other places that speak more clearly.[8]

Here we are reminded that it is unwise to ground doctrine on obscure passages of Scripture. Clearer passages of the Bible will explain the more obscure passages. Scripture will not contradict itself, so God, the maker and giver of brains, expects us to do the hard thinking required to reconcile all of what the Bible says about a particular subject. If my Mormon friends had followed this advice, I'm sure they would not have made Proverbs 8 their go-to text in support of their doctrine of pre-existence.

2) History Solves Mystery

Just as words should be interpreted in their *grammatical* context, they should also be interpreted in their *historical* context. The authors of the Bible wrote to an audience that would understand many of their references without much explanation. The Bible refers to places, people, customs, and circumstances that the original readers immediately grasped. Readers of the same words thousands of years later and thousands of miles away, however, need to study the historical context of that era to understand the meaning.

For example, Christians today in North America may not understand why Paul wrote the book of Philippians from a Roman prison because we have nothing to fear in North America when we confess that "Jesus is Lord." This was not the case for Christians in the first century. Subjects of the Roman Empire were required to annually state their allegiance to Caesar by bowing their knee and confessing that "Caesar is Lord." They could worship other gods if they wanted, but the official state religion was Caesar worship, the imperial cult. Most of the Caesars were deified after death, but a few insisted on being worshipped as a god even while they were still alive. During

8. 1:9.

the lifetimes of the New Testament authors, refusal to make this confession was a crime, an act of treason against Rome.

With this bit of history, it means that much more when we read in Philippians that "at the name of Jesus every knee should bow, in heaven and on earth and under the earth, and every tongue confess that Jesus Christ is Lord, to the glory of the Father" (Phil 2:10). Caesar is not sovereign over the universe. He is under the authority of Jesus Christ, whose name is "above every name" (2:9), even the name of Caesar.

Paul plainly preached that "Jesus Christ is Lord," God in the flesh, the King of kings risen from the dead, and for that reason he was considered a threat to the state and was writing the Philippians from a Roman prison (Phil 1:4). The Philippians are concerned that Paul's imprisonment will stop the advance of the gospel, but Paul writes to assure them the gospel will advance no matter what Caesar or anyone else does to stop it. While Caesar may be lord of some, "Jesus is Lord of lords" (Rev 17:14). Knowing this history helps solve the mystery.

3) Reason Gets Results

When God speaks to us in his Word, he will speak clearly and logically, "For God is not a God of confusion but of peace" (1 Cor 14:33). God has an orderly mind. He is a reasonable God who speaks intelligibly. Therefore, Christians must do all things "decently and in order" (1 Cor 14:40). "All things" includes listening to God. God's logic is impeccable and we should strive to be like him in this. So as you study the Bible, keep in mind that God cannot contradict himself or be inconsistent.

The Bible is full of difficult passages that you will find hard to reconcile. That is not the Bible's problem, but ours. We are far removed from the culture, customs, and language of the original authors and their audience, which makes some things harder to understand. Still, there will usually be several possible solutions for these problems in the Bible.

First, remember from our discussion on context that the unclear or ambiguous passages should be interpreted in light of the clear and unambiguous passages. It is never wise to build doctrine on an unclear passage.

Next, become familiar with some common logical fallacies that we tend to commit in our thinking. Americans have largely lost the ability to think clearly, our brains pickled in political attack ads, beer commercial nonsense, and radio talk show bluster. And most university majors require no formal training in logic and philosophy. So every Christian needs to take some time to train his or her mind to think like a good lawyer and listen like a wise judge.

One day I was digging up some old bushes in our front yard. I labored for an hour or two with a shovel in the July heat and began to wonder if there was a better way. About that time I glanced over at my pickup truck in the driveway and got an idea. I tied one end of a rope to my trailer hitch and one end to the bush, hit the gas, and extracted the bush in seconds. In comparison to me, my truck is strong. What if I tried the same procedure with the massive hickory tree in my backyard? I would quickly come to the conclusion that my truck is not strong. So here are two statements:

My truck is strong

My truck is not strong

Are these two statements in contradiction? Not really. About the law of non-contradiction, R.C. Sproul writes that "A cannot be A and non-A (-A) at the same time and in the same relationship. Something can be A and B at the same time but not in the same relationship. I can be a father (A) and a son (B) but not in the same relationship [I am a father to my son but a son to my father]."[9]

So on the surface, it appears that my statements are contradictory, but there is no actual contradiction because my truck is strong and not strong at different times and in different relationships. In relationship to a bush, my truck is strong (A). In relationship to a tree, it is not strong (B). However, if I said that relative to one particular bush my truck is both strong (A) and not strong (-A), that would be a contradiction. In that case, the truck can't be both.

Likewise, there will be many statements in the Bible that will seem like an *apparent* contradiction, but on closer examination, you will find these statements are not an *actual* contradiction. For example, Jesus consistently taught his disciples to pursue a policy of non-violence. In no case were they to use physical force to advance his cause. The gospel must be spread only through the persuasive preaching of Christ-followers who are willing to love, serve, suffer, and perhaps die for the Christian faith, but they are not to inflict suffering or death on others in order to impose the gospel. At his arrest, Jesus told Peter not to resist the authorities but to put his sword back

9. Sproul, *Not a Chance*, 12.

in its sheath (John 18:11). At his trial, Jesus was clear that if his kingdom was of this world, his "servants would have been fighting" (John 18:36).

At one point Jesus said, "I did not come to bring peace, but a sword" (Matt 10:34). On the surface, this seems like a contradiction:

> Jesus taught his disciples to use a sword (A).

> Jesus taught his disciples to not use a sword (non-A).

In the context of Matthew 10, however, it is clear that Jesus is speaking figuratively. He is not telling his disciples to grab a sword and start beheading their religious opponents. Rather, he is saying that if his disciples continue to follow him, they will be hated, disowned by their culture, even by their own families. The sword is a metaphor for the truth of God's word (Eph 6:17; Heb 4:12). Jesus' preaching would divide friends, families, and countrymen because some would believe him and some would not. Now the propositions look like this:

> Jesus taught his disciples to use a figurative sword (A).

> Jesus taught his disciples to not use a literal sword (B).

Jesus' instruction is still binding on his followers today. Throughout church history, many professing Christians have ignored Jesus' clear prohibition of violence in spreading the gospel, ripping Matthew 10:34 out of its context. If they had only listened carefully to God in his Word, much reproach on Christianity could have been avoided.

An *argument from silence* is a conclusion based on silence or lack of contrary evidence. An argument from silence is not always a fallacy, but when an argument from silence is the primary evidence, it is often a fallacy. And when an argument from silence contradicts the clearer existing evidence, it is almost always a fallacy.

Sometimes an argument from silence is acceptable. In *Silver Blaze*, Sherlock Holmes was able to solve a crime because of a non-barking dog. The question is this: Who stole Colonel Ross's racehorse? The prime suspect is the owner of the stable, of course, because the stable dog never barked when the crime took place. The dog only barks at intruders.[10] So an argument from silence is not always a fallacy. Sometimes, it can be added as corroborating evidence.

---

10. Doyle, *Memoirs of Sherlock Holmes*, 23.

For example, in order to make their case for blessing same-sex marriage, some church leaders have drawn attention to the silence of Jesus on homosexuality. "Jesus never said anything about it," we are told, as if that somehow settles the argument. First, we don't know that Jesus "never said anything about it." All we know is that there is no written record of Jesus specifically commenting on homosexuality. Actually, there is no account of Jesus commenting about a lot of things. There is no written record of Jesus condemning rape, the molestation of children, or sex with horses. What are we to conclude from this silence? Maybe, sometimes, some things are so obvious that they just don't need to be said.

On this same issue, the argument from silence can be used as corroborating evidence *against* same-sex marriage. In all of Scripture there is not one positive and God-pleasing example of a homosexual relationship. The dog doesn't bark. At the same time, there are several clear prohibitions of homosexual conduct.[11] If God is in favor of same-sex marriage, it is hard to imagine why he would never say so. An argument from silence, then, can be used as corroborating evidence, but it becomes a fallacy when it has no other supporting evidence or it clearly contradicts existing evidence.

In a *false dilemma*, sometimes called the fallacy of the excluded middle, we erroneously reduce the amount of possible options or alternatives to answer a question. For example, according to the atheist Sam Harris, the case of the sea of cast metal in 2 Chronicles 4:2 is an example of a mathematical error in the Bible.[12] This piece of furniture in the Temple held water used for the ritual bathing of the priests, and the dimensions are given in the text.

The Bible reports it is about 180 inches in diameter. You may remember from high school geometry that the circumference of a circle is pi x D (3.14 x the diameter) which would mean the circumference of the bowl should be 565 inches. However, the text reports that the circumference is about 540 inches. Critics like Harris say that there are two options only. Either this standard formula used in geometry is wrong or the Bible is wrong. Since no one will concede the mathematical formula is wrong, we must conclude the Bible is wrong. But is this a true dilemma?

11. Gen 19:1–11; Lev 18:22; 20:13; Judg 19:16–24; 1 Kgs 14:24; 15:12; 2 Kgs 23:7; Rom 1:18–32; 1 Cor 6:9–11; 1 Tim 1:8–10; Jude 7. In addition, Jesus clearly defines marriage as heterosexual, monogamous, and permanent in Matthew 19:4–6. Since sex is permitted only for a married couple, this definition of marriage prohibits all homosexual activity.

12. Harris, *Letter to Christian Nation*, 60–61.

Actually several middle options are available. For example, perhaps the Bible is speaking in approximate numbers and we are placing unreasonable expectations of precision on the text. Whenever we speak of the dimensions of furniture or even our own house, we rarely use precise measurements. When we bought our present house, the realtor told us it was 1900 square feet. Really? Exactly 1900? Not 1890 or 1910 or 1900.25? Are those inside dimensions or outside? No one believes it is exactly 1900 square feet, not even Sam Harris. We all know this is an approximation and we do not consider the realtor to be a liar. That is just normal human language.

Another intriguing possibility is suggested in the context where we are told the metal bowl was four inches thick (2 Chr 4:5). By measuring the inside diameter, you shave 8 inches off of the diameter. In this case, pi x D would equal 540.08 inches.[13] I'm still not sure which option is correct, but I know this: To interpret 2 Chronicles 4 in a way that makes the Bible speak error is to commit the logical fallacy of false dilemma.

By now you might see that no one is asking for special treatment when it comes to interpreting the Bible. The same rules of interpretation apply for any written document. These are the first three rules of interpretation. In the next chapter, we will add four more.

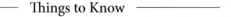

Things to Know

- What are the first 3 rules of interpretation?

13. Lindsell, *Battle for the Bible*, 165–66.

8

Sharpening Your Listening Skills

I studied and restudied the Scriptures to see if the traditional understanding of those verses that condemned homosexuality really meant what I had been taught they meant . . . On January 1, 2010, Mark became my legal husband in marriage.

–GENE ROBINSON, BISHOP, EPISCOPAL CHURCH[1]

And yet it is not lawful for the Church to ordain any thing that is contrary to God's Word written, neither may it so expound one place of Scripture, that it be repugnant to another.

–CHURCH OF ENGLAND, *THE THIRTY-NINE ARTICLES*, 1571[2]

ALL OF US, AT times, hear only what we want to hear. And too often, what we hear is not at all what was said. We are selectively deaf to inconvenient truth. So we convince ourselves that what we just heard is not what was said because, well, we want to do what we want to do. This is all the more reason to take the time to sharpen our listening skills, especially when we are listening to God. To help you become a better listener, consider four more rules of interpretation.

4) Inference Makes a Difference

As followers of Christ in the twenty-first century, many matters that concern us are not specifically addressed in Scripture. This is where inference can help us in understanding the Bible. Inference refers to a conclusion that is reached on the basis of evidence and reasoning. You may reach a

1. Robinson, *God Believes in Love*, 7, 14.
2. Article 20.

conclusion about God's will that is not specifically articulated in Scripture but is a reasonable inference from the precepts and principles of Scripture.

Jesus uses the rule of inference in Luke 20:37–38 when he is arguing against the Sadducees, who denied life after death and thus, bodily resurrection. Jesus takes them to an unlikely text in Exodus 3:6, saying that "even Moses showed in the passage about the bush, where he calls the Lord the God of Abraham and the God of Isaac and the God of Jacob. How he is not God of the dead, but of the living, for all live to him." Exodus 3 is not specifically about the resurrection, but Jesus seizes on the tense of the verbs and makes an inference. God did not say to Moses, "I *was* the God of Abraham" but rather "I *am* the God of Abraham" because Abraham (who had died centuries earlier) was present with God, awaiting a future resurrection. This is an inference from the text.

If God had addressed every single issue in his written revelation that every believer in every generation would ever face, the book would be impractically enormous. That doesn't mean he cannot speak through his Word to every single issue you encounter. While there may be no specific directives on a given subject, it is possible to draw out timeless principles that can apply in many kinds of situations if we just think about it.

We often don't want to think about it because our hearts are deceitful (Jer 17:9). To be honest, we are looking for loopholes. Deep down, we may know that a course of action is wrong, but we still want to go there anyway. If that particular thing is not addressed in the Bible we might rationalize that it must be okay with God.

Take the emotionally charged issue of abortion for example. Someone might conclude that since the Bible never uses the word "abortion" that God approves of it. Besides the argument from silence, notice the suppression of evidence. When Mary and Elizabeth were both pregnant, Mary came to visit her. When Mary greeted her, we are told that "the baby leaped" in Elizabeth's womb (Luke 1:41). She then tells Mary, "the baby in my womb leaped for joy" (Luke 1:44). The word for "baby" used here is the same word used to describe the very born Jesus as he was "lying in the manger" (Luke 2:16). Elizabeth, Luke (the human author), and God (the divine Author) all agree that the unborn John the Baptist was in fact a baby. So the Bible never specifically addresses abortion, but we can reach a solid interpretation and application by way of inference.

Premise #1: The Bible (A) prohibits killing innocent human life (B)

Premise #2: An unborn baby (C) is innocent human life (B)

Therefore: The Bible (A) prohibits killing unborn babies (C).

5) Spirit-Reliance Gives Guidance

Some would argue that this should be first on the list. I don't disagree, but you will see in a moment why I put it here. Others would argue that this principle only applies to interpreting the Bible. Not really. I try to apply this even when I am interpreting the words of my wife. As a Christian, I want and need the Holy Spirit's help in discerning and interpreting all truth. When I read a newspaper or an email from a friend, I need the Holy Spirit's help, but I especially need his help in interpreting the most important written communication in all of history.

By Spirit-dependence, I mean that we should come to each passage of the Bible prayerfully, relying on the Holy Spirit to be our lead teacher who guides us into all truth. Ask him to remove your bias and request him to overpower your flawed presuppositions. "Now we have received not the spirit of the world, but the Spirit who is from God, that we might understand the things freely given us by God" (1 Cor 2:12). This ministry of the Holy Spirit is one of God's many gifts to the believer. The unbeliever, on the other hand, "does not accept the things of the Spirit of God, for they are folly to him, and he is not able to understand them because they are spiritually discerned" (1Cor 2:14). This is why Christians throughout history, in agreement with the Westminster Confession, "acknowledge the inward illumination of the Spirit of God to be necessary for the saving understanding of such things as are revealed in the Word."[3]

As you read and think about the words of the Bible, ask the Holy Spirit to "guide you into all truth" (John 16:13). One of the key rules of interpretation is to recognize your own intellectual frailty and your immeasurable dependence on the Holy Spirit's ministry of illumination.

3. 1:6.

6) Type of Literature Gives a Clearer Picture

The type (or genre) of literature affects the way you will interpret the text. Each genre has a special set of guidelines that you will need to keep in mind.

A huge portion of the Bible is *historical* narrative, which means it is filled with great stories. It tells us about real people and events in the unfolding drama of God's redemption. The historical sections of the Bible report the facts, but not necessarily all the facts. The authors of Scripture, like all historians, are selective in details they provide. And, like all historians, they don't always arrange their material in strict chronological order, but sometimes by topics or themes.

Historical narrative tells us the way things were, but not necessarily how they should be. That's why it is unwise to build doctrine solely on a foundation of historical narrative. For example, as you read the Gospels and Acts it seems like everywhere you look people are speaking in tongues, healing the sick, and raising the dead. These historical books report what happened in the ministries of Jesus and the apostles, but that doesn't necessarily mean these things are normative for the church today.

Another large percentage of the Bible is *poetry*. Poetry is the language of the heart that was easy to memorize (in the original language of Hebrew) because of its rhymes and meter. It is often put to music. In fact, one book of the Bible, Psalms, is a collection of 150 songs.

Poetry has "poetic license" to exaggerate and generalize. Solomon writes that "the plans of the diligent lead surely to abundance, but everyone who is hasty comes only to poverty" (Prov 21:5). Yet we all know good people who made sound business plans and worked hard, but due to unforeseen events, the business failed. However, most people who have ever built a profitable business got there as a result of good plans and hard work. The general principle is that the most likely way to avoid poverty is to plan your work and work your plan.

Poetry plays with words to connect emotionally and paint memorable mental pictures. "Like a gold ring in a pig's snout," says Proverbs 11:22, "is a woman who shows no discretion." And notice how much of the Bible's poetry follows a form called parallelism.

| Like a gold ring | in a | pig's snout, |
| Is a beautiful woman | who shows | no discretion. |

Another sizable section of the Bible is a kind of literature called *prophecy*. Prophecy often predicts events before they happen, and these books can also contain historical and poetic sections. Prophecy was given to encourage God's people when they were down and discipline God's people when they were rebellious. When his people are in a season of despair, God speaks through the prophets to give them hope for the future. God knows the future because he controls it and occasionally in his Word, he pulls back the curtain to give us a glimpse of things to come. Much of prophecy involves highly symbolic language that is often not fully understood until after the prediction has been fulfilled.

A distinct form of literature in the New Testament is a collection of *letters,* sometimes called epistles, written by apostles. Most of the letters are written to entire churches, but a few are very personal and directed to a specific individual. The great value of these letters is that they are didactic in nature. That is, their purpose is to teach. For example, while the historical narrative material of Acts accurately reports how things *were* in the church, the teaching material of the New Testament letters instruct us on how things *ought to be* in the church.

The letters were written by the apostles specifically to teach the church on a wide assortment of issues pertaining to what Christians should believe and how they should behave. These letters, then, have greater weight in forming doctrine. The teaching literature, such as Romans, interprets the historical literature such as Acts. While the teaching literature is mainly *prescriptive*, the historical literature is mainly *descriptive*.

In all the genres of the Bible, you will encounter *figures of speech*. Once again, this is just a normal part of human language. It's probably been a while since you studied this, so here are a few examples to remind you.

Metaphors are comparisons that do not use the words *as* or *like*. When Jesus said, "I am the gate" (John 10:9), he obviously did not mean he was wood and hinges. And when he held out the bread to his disciples at the Last Supper and said, "This is my body" (Matt 26:26) it should be clear that Jesus did not intend to mean the bread literally became (or would become) his flesh. Jesus is speaking metaphorically.

Similes are comparisons that use the words *as* or *like*. When Paul says "we were gentle among you, like a nursing mother taking care of her children" (1 Thess 2:7), he paints a beautiful picture of the ministry, tenderly nurturing and protecting new Christians. Similes are usually easy to recognize.

We all use *hyperbole* when we intentionally exaggerate to emphasize a point. When we read that "all the country of Judea and Jerusalem were going out" (Mark 1:5) to be baptized by John the Baptist, we would err to think that means every single person in that region was baptized by John. It means a lot of people from all over the region were responding to his message and being baptized.

Idioms are figures of speech that often suggest a lack of scientific precision. We are told that some women came to the tomb on the morning Jesus was raised from the dead "when the sun had risen" (Mark 16:2). Here in the twenty-first century, we know that the sun does not literally rise, but even in the twenty-first century we use this idiom when we tell our friends we will meet them at the golf course at sunrise.

How will you remember these rules?

Context is king.
History reveals mystery.
Reason gets results.
Inference makes a difference.
Spirit-dependence gives guidance.
Type of literature paints a clearer picture.

7) Christ is Central

By now you may have noticed that the first six principles are framed in the acrostic CHRIST. That should help you remember the seventh principle: Christ is central to the whole Bible. Jesus said of the Old Testament Scriptures that "they bear witness about me" (John 5:39). The Bible is all about Jesus, from beginning to end.

One of the earliest references to Jesus in the Bible is found in Genesis 3:15: "And he shall bruise your head." Sometimes called the "the first gospel" (Latin, *protoevangelium*), this is God's earliest promise that a descendant of Eve will bring deliverance to fallen man. The last reference to Jesus in the Bible is in the last verse of the last chapter of the last book. The Bible ends with this blessing: "The grace of the Lord Jesus be with all. Amen" (Rev 22:21).

In between Genesis and Revelation, you will find that every book is about Jesus. The Old Testament poetry speaks of the anguish of his crucifixion a thousand years before it happened (Ps 22). The Old Testament prophets predicted his birth, even that it would be in Bethlehem (Mic 5:2). So the Old Testament predicts his coming, the Gospels report his coming (Luke 1:1–4), and the rest of the New Testament explains what he accomplished by coming (1 Tim 1:15). The Bible is the written record of how God *created* all things through Jesus Christ (Col 1:16) and how God *redeems* fallen man through Jesus Christ (Col 1:14). Therefore, any interpretation of the Bible that denies or limits the complete humanity, full deity, and total supremacy of Jesus Christ is a false interpretation.

A Word of Caution—Beware of Private Interpretation

After you read and think about a passage of Scripture, you will develop an interpretation. Have you heard God correctly? It is always wise to get confirmation. You are not the first person to read this text or attempt an interpretation. You are not in uncharted territory, and you would be wise to learn from the experience of those who have gone before you. If other Christians in previous generations heard what you heard, you will get stronger confirmation that you heard correctly.

You should be alarmed if you are the first person to hold an innovative interpretation of Scripture. It would seem odd for God to say something to you in a text that he has said to no one else in history. It is unlikely that for two thousand years, everyone, including some of the best minds in history, got it wrong, but you have finally gotten it right. You should not completely trust yourself as you listen to God in Scripture. You bring personal prejudices to the text. Like the rest of us, you are biased and highly influenced by your culture. You will tend to force the words of the Bible into your preconceived ideas. You will be inclined to rationalize your current course of action. You will see things that are not there, and not see things that are, because you are used to a certain way of thinking. That is why you need confirmation. Where do you get it?

Most pastors I know love it when people in their church bring them questions about the Bible. This is why most of us became pastors! Many of us pursued formal training to increase our competence in the Scripture so we could help others understand it and apply it to their lives. Hopefully, your pastor loves God's word and can give you confirmation of whether or not you are on the right track.

Even if your pastor is competent, he is not always present. In fact, good pastors will expect you to learn how to feed yourself from the Word and in turn feed others, especially your children. Training you to do this is your pastor's job (2 Tim 2:2). One way you can feed yourself is by consulting good commentaries and study Bibles. The best commentators are aware of how Christians have understood the Bible throughout the centuries. Consequently, historic precedent will inform their interpretation.

Every Christian ought to know how to listen to God in the Bible. If you can do this, you will become more competent. By becoming more competent, you will increase your credibility as an ambassador of Jesus Christ, not only to the world, but to your children.

Now we turn to the next step in becoming a credible man: learning how to think about God.

Things to Know

- What are the 7 rules of interpretation?

9

Do We Still Need the Creed?

God forbid that he should have a son!

−KORAN[1]

I believe in God the Father
   Almighty, Creator of heaven and earth,
I believe in Jesus Christ,
   his only Son, our Lord.
   He was conceived by the power of the Holy Spirit and
   born of the virgin Mary.
   He suffered under Pontius Pilate, was
   crucified, died, and was buried.
   On the third day, he rose again.
   He ascended into heaven, and is
   seated at the right hand of the Father.
   He will come again to judge the living and the dead.
I believe in the Holy Spirit
   the holy Christian church,
   the communion of the saints,
   the forgiveness of sins,
   the resurrection of the body, and the
   life everlasting. Amen.

−THE APOSTLES' CREED[2]

1. 4:171.

2. The form of Apostles' Creed we have today is not exactly the form that Christians used in the 2nd century. The form of the 2nd century creed, sometimes called the *Old Roman Creed,* or *The Roman Symbol,* has similar structure but less detail. Over the years, nothing of substance was subtracted but some things were added as the creed evolved.

THE PROPHET MUHAMMAD, FOUNDER of Islam, had an opportunity to become a Christian. Sort of. Born six centuries after Jesus, Muhammad, early in his life, came into contact with professing Christians who tried to explain the trinity, one of the most difficult doctrines of the Christian faith. They apparently taught that God had sexual intercourse with the virgin Mary resulting in the conception of Jesus. They emphasized how the virgin birth and miracles Jesus performed proved he was the Son of God. When they tried to put it all together, they presented three gods to Muhammad, a form of polytheism. Muhammad mistakenly thought that real Christians believed in three separate gods.[3] And for the rest of his life, Muhammad rejected what he thought was Christianity.

Muhammad didn't reject all of what he heard. To this day, Muslims believe in the virgin birth of Jesus and agree that he was a great miracle-working prophet who spoke for God. Though they believe he is inferior to the prophet Muhammad, they hold Jesus in high regard as a prophet, but the vestiges of Muhammad's run-in with heretical Christians are forever embedded in the Muslim holy book. "So believe in God," states the Koran, "and his apostles and do not say 'Three.' Forbear and it should be better for you. God forbid that he should have a son!"[4] And again, "Unbelievers are those who say, 'God is one of three.' There is but one God. If they do not desist from so saying, those of them that disbelieve shall be surely punished."[5] And Muslims have been punishing Christians ever since, in obedience to their founder's example and their sacred scripture. Unfortunately, Christians have too often punished right back, even though their founder specifically forbids them to do so.[6] The sad misunderstanding

---

The general form we use today goes back to at least the fourth century. You may be familiar with a different version, perhaps with more archaic language. For example, you may have learned that Jesus is coming back to judge "the quick and the dead." We will use a version that reflects changes in the English language so that it reads "the living and the dead." Others may notice the absence of Jesus descending into hell. This version removes that because it was not in the earliest versions of the Old Roman Creed (see Marcellus's translation in Pelikan, *Creeds and Confessions*, 1:682). Finally, some may notice that "the holy catholic church" is replaced by "holy Christian church" following the lead of the Lutheran Church to avoid confusion between "the holy catholic (universal) church" and "the Roman Catholic Church." The form I am using here is adapted from McGrath, *I Believe*, 8.

3. George, *Is the Father*, 58–59.
4. Koran, 4:171.
5. Koran, 5:73.
6. I have addressed this issue in greater detail in *Which "Real" Jesus?* 112–47.

between Muslims and Christians has been a source of hostile, and often bloody, global conflict for fourteen centuries now. And it all began with thinking about God the wrong way.

The Apostles' Creed

There is a right way to think about God and countless wrong ways to think about God. When we believe things about God that are not true, we are not thinking about him in the right way, and that is a problem in itself. The problem is compounded when we say what we think. When we talk about God to our children, our friends, and our neighbors, we reveal what we think about God. So if we do not think correctly about God, we will eventually slander God. The old word that people used to use for slandering God is *blasphemy*. Blasphemy is a breathtakingly serious offense with immeasurably tragic consequences.

As we have seen, God has revealed himself to us in the written Word, so if we want to think correctly about God, our mind must be informed by the Bible. Because the Bible is a big book, Christians in the past have summarized the Bible as a way of helping each generation remember core truths about God. These succinct statements of belief are sometimes called creeds, which comes from a Latin word that means "I believe."

Most scholars agree that one of the earliest Christian creeds is found in Galatians 4:4–7.

God
>   sent forth his

Son
>   born of a woman
>   born under the law
>   to redeem those who were under the law
>   so we might receive adoption as sons.
>   And because you are sons,
>   God has sent the

Spirit
>   of his Son into our hearts,
>   crying, "Abba! Father!"

The next generation of Christians followed this structure and filled it in with more detail from God's Word. This became the main tool to teach new believers and prepare them for baptism. At their baptism, they would then be asked to confess what they believed about God. At that point, they would recite an earlier form of what we call today the Apostles' Creed. The apostles themselves did not write this creed and it is not inspired Scripture. Rather, it is a succinct summary of the apostles' teaching composed by the early church.

"I Don't Need No Creed!"

Already, some of you are on high alert. You don't trust creeds. Maybe you grew up in a church that rejected them as man-made traditions or saw them as barriers to heart-felt worship. That's understandable because in many Christian traditions, reciting the creed is just passionless parroting of empty words. And creeds are not necessary for your salvation. "You do not become a Christian by reciting a creed," notes Alister McGrath, "rather, the creed provides a useful summary of the main points of your faith."[7] Creeds are like anything that is of great value. They can be misused, neglected, underappreciated, and discarded. In the end, though, you will find that creeds are inescapable.

How so? Take for instance the Christian who rejects the use of creeds, saying, "No creed but the Bible!" His statement is itself a creed. It is a succinct summary of what he believes, namely that he doesn't need a creed because he has a Bible. Or take for example a Christian who rejects creeds because they become repetitive as some churches recite them in worship Sunday after Sunday. Yet the same Christian doesn't mind singing *Amazing Grace* more than once in his life. Why does it make a difference whether you say or sing your creed?

So these are the two things you need to know about creeds. First, you need to know that creeds are succinct statements of belief. Second, you need to know that creeds are inescapable.

The What-Ifs of History

History is filled with what-ifs. What if Lee had not lost Jackson at Chancellorsville? What if the rescue had failed at Dunkirk? What if Lincoln had insisted on tighter security at Ford's Theater? What if Jack Ruby had not shot Lee Harvey Oswald? What if Werner Von Braun had gone to the Soviet

---

7. McGrath, *I Believe*, 14.

Union instead of the United States? What if Julius Caesar had not crossed the Rubicon? Add this to the list: What if Muhammad had encountered genuine Christians who knew how to think correctly about God and explain the three chief articles of the Apostles' Creed and the doctrine of the trinity? In the following chapters, we will take some time to unpack the Apostles' Creed and learn how to think more clearly about God.

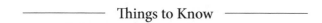

Things to Know

- What are 2 things every Christian man ought to know about creeds?

---

10 ———

I Believe

I believe in God and his son, Jesus. Do you?

−L'IL WAYNE, RAPPER[1]

Question 24: How are these articles divided? Into three parts: The first concerns
God the Father and our creation; the second, God the Son and our redemption;
and the third, God the Holy Spirit and our sanctification.

−HEIDELBERG CATECHISM, 1563

TAKE A DEEP BREATH before you enter this chapter. Like a good steak, you
will need to cut the Apostles' Creed into manageable pieces before you chew
on it. Notice, first, the singular form of God. The creed does not say, I believe in Gods. Rather, it says, I believe in God. There is one God, there is no
other, and he has no rivals. This is a point of agreement we Christians have
with Jews and Muslims. We are monotheists. We believe in only one God.
Surely, "the Lord our God, the Lord is one" (Deut 6:4). If "you believe that
God is one; you do well" (Jas 2:19). And this one God has done three mar-
velous things for us. For centuries Christians have noted that the Apostles'
Creed is divided into three chief articles that declare God's three gracious
acts on our behalf. The first article is *creation*, the second is *redemption*, and
the third is *sanctification*.

God is the One Who Created Everything

To believe in "God the Father Almighty" is to affirm at least three things
about God. First, God is smart, so he always *knows* what is best for his

1. Sanneh, "Savoring a Moment."

children. The big theological word for this attribute of God is omniscience. Only God knows everything and in our praises to him we agree that he is "the only wise God" (Rom 16:27). Second, God is strong, so he is always *able* to do what is best for his children. Therefore, we can say to God, "In your hand are power and might, so that none is able to withstand you" (2 Chr 20:6). Theologians sometimes refer to this as God's omnipotence. God can do anything he wants to do. Third, God is good, so he always *does* what is best for his children. Here we are speaking of God's benevolence and the Bible affirms repeatedly that "for those who love God all things work together for good" (Rom 8:28).

That does not mean that all the things that happen to Christians *feel* good. There will be times in every Christian's life when he or she will doubt God's omniscience, question his omnipotence, or even deny his benevolence. We may reason that either God is smart, but not strong; or strong, but not smart; or strong and smart, but not good. What other way is there to explain why I am suffering like this? When we think about God like that, we are not thinking correctly.

Every parent reading this book knows that there are times when we must intentionally inflict or permit some pain in our children's lives for their ultimate good. In their early years, even if we explain the purpose of the pain, they would not understand what we are doing. So, just as our earthly fathers "disciplined us and we respected them," so too, "God disciplines us for our good, that we may share his holiness. For the moment all discipline seems painful rather than pleasant" (Heb 12:9–11) but God, our Father, knows what he is doing. Just like you don't always give your children what they ask for because you love them, neither does God the Father (Matt 7:9–11).

Our heavenly father is also our Creator. When the Bible uses the phrase "heaven and earth," it means everything (Eph 3:9). God created everything out of nothing. When your children ask *But who created God?*, the answer is simple: no one. God is not a created being. He is the uncreated Creator who eternally existed in the past and will continue to exist eternally in the future.

The Bible is clear on the fact *that* God made everything, but it is more silent than we might prefer on the details about *how* and *when* he did it. Many Christians today are working hard to reconcile the knowledge we are gaining in science with the knowledge we have in the Scripture, and there is room for various views among believers who love the Bible. In the end, however, there will be no final conflict between the study of God's world (good science) and the study of God's word (good theology).

Knowing that God is the creator and sustainer of all things leads Christians to give thanks for all he has provided. He has made us and given us the ability to think, attend school, and work. He has given us our food, our clothes, and our homes—every good thing that goes *in* us, every good thing that goes *on* us, and every good thing that goes *around* us. He created all of these good things for us and gives them to us even though we don't deserve them. Therefore, they ought "to be received with thanksgiving by those who believe and know the truth" (1 Tim 4:3).

God is the One Who Redeems Sinners

The second article focuses on "Jesus Christ, his only son, our Lord." Jesus is God's "only son" (John 3:16). There is no other. "But," you may ask, "if God is our Father and we are his children, how can Jesus be 'his only son'?" The word for "only" here means that Jesus is "one of a kind" and there is no one like him. Unlike us, Jesus was not created, for Jesus has always existed and always will. Jesus was there with God the Father at creation and "by him all things were created in heaven and earth" (Col 1:16).

To say that Jesus is the Son of God is to say that Jesus is God. "Lord" is the title of deity (Rom 10:13). Jesus said the sort of things only God can say (Matt 11:10; John 5:18), did the sort of things only God can do (John 11:33–34), and received worship that only God should receive (John 20:28). His resurrection validates the claims he made for himself, and therefore his followers came to believe that Jesus is God (John 1:1, 14).

This article of the creed also asserts that Jesus is man, born of the virgin Mary. As a fully human man, he experienced real suffering under the Roman governor Pilate. Jesus felt every bit of the profound emotional and physical suffering that was a Roman crucifixion. And when Jesus died, his heart really stopped beating and all brainwaves ended.

So Jesus was both God and man. He did not cease to be God in order to become man. He did not exchange his deity for humanity. Rather he added humanity to his deity (Phil 2:5–7). Jesus had to be both God and man because his job required it. We don't have to guess about why Jesus came to earth. Paul clearly states that "Jesus Christ came into the world to save sinners" (1 Tim 1:15) and he saved sinners by serving as the only "mediator between God and men" (1 Tim 2:5). Being God, he could represent

God to man, and being man he could represent man to God in this, the greatest of all disputes.

This miracle of God becoming flesh is sometimes called the "incarnation." By becoming a man, the Son of God was able to purchase us from the penalty of our sins with his own blood (Acts 20:28). That's what redemption means. God redeemed us, bought us, with the blood of his only son. This is the job that Jesus came to do, and when he had done it, he could say, "It is finished" (John 19:30). For that reason, heavenly beings sing to Jesus, "you were slain, and by your blood you ransomed people for God" (Rev 5:9).

Because God is just, he is self-compelled to punish sin. Because God is merciful, he is self-compelled to forgive sin. This seems like an impasse because he cannot do both. Yet God found a way by providing a morally perfect and totally willing substitute to die in our place and take our punishment. Only God is perfect and only man can die, so God became a man and the only acceptable sacrifice for our sins. Through the incarnation, God preserves both his justice and mercy.

After his resurrection, Jesus ascended into heaven (Acts 1:9) and is now seated at the right hand of the Father, a place of highest honor (Heb 2:7-9). There he serves as our advocate, arguing our case and defending us against all accusations (1 John 2:1), and so we Christians pray in the name of Jesus.

One day, he will leave that seat and return to the earth in order to bring to full completion his plan of redemption. His primary function at this "second coming" will be as a judge. For those who have been redeemed, there is no need to fear this judgment. If you are a true Christian, Jesus, your judge, is also your advocate. However, for those who denied the Son of God, refusing his mediation between them and God, this judgment will be unspeakably tragic as they "give an account to him who is ready to judge the living and the dead" (1 Pet 4:5).

The end of the Bible is a lot like the beginning. Just as we don't know exactly when God created the heavens and earth, Christians don't know exactly when Jesus will return. For that reason you must always be ready, "for you know neither the day nor the hour" (Matt 25:13). Believers today often disagree on the sequence and order of events leading up to when Jesus will come again, but all agree on this: Jesus is coming again. He came the first time as a Lamb, but he will come again as Lion. He came the first time as a suffering servant, but he will come again as a conquering king. He came the first time to be judged by pompous men, but he will come again to judge the living and the dead.

God is the One Who Sanctifies the Redeemed

When we say we believe in the Holy Spirit, we are affirming first of all that the Holy Spirit is a person. In fact, he is always referred to with masculine pronouns. He is not an impersonal force or power or an "it." As a person, he can be grieved (Eph 4:30), lied to (Acts 5:3), and resisted (Acts 7:51). He can select and organize leaders (Acts 20:28), speak (Acts 28:25), and serve as an eyewitness (Acts 5:32). To think about God the Holy Spirit as an impersonal force is to think about him incorrectly.

God did not redeem us with the blood of his Son to leave us as we are. Now that we can approach him boldly in Jesus' name (Heb 4:16), God expects us to start acting like Jesus. That work of cleaning us up, making us holy, and forming our character belongs to God the Holy Spirit.

The Holy Spirit is not only a person. He is also God (Acts 5:4). He is God the Spirit who makes us holy. The word that means "to make holy" is sanctify. The process of making someone holy is called sanctification.

That sanctification does not come all at once. It begins when the Holy Spirit gives you spiritual life, enabling you to believe in the Son. You would not be able to believe in him otherwise (John 3:3–7). From that point, the Holy Spirit begins a process that will transform you into the character of Jesus (Rom 8:29). There are some traits of Jesus that belong only to God, like omnipotence and omnipresence. These traits will never be yours, but the moral qualities of Jesus, like love and kindness and self-control, will become more evident in your life. You will not become like Jesus overnight. Rather, it is a progressive, life-long process that does not end until you die. Every day requires vigilance and struggle, which is why the Christian life can be considered "the good fight" (2 Tim 4:7). Some days will be better than others in this protracted battle. Like the stock market, you will be up and down in the effort to become more like Christ, but over the long term, by God's grace, you will be more up than down. And finally, when you die or he comes again, you will be transformed to be like him (1 John 3:2).

God the Holy Spirit has given us many gifts to aid us in our sanctification. The remainder of the Apostles' Creed describes the means by which the Holy Spirit makes us holy. Luther's Larger Catechism says that the Holy Spirit "leads us into His holy congregation, and places us in the bosom of the Church, whereby he preaches to us and brings us to Christ."[2]

2. *Book of Concord*, Luther's Large Catechism, "The Apostles' Creed."

So here is a compressed explanation of the rest of the Creed: The Holy Spirit uses the church to bring about our eventual and total sanctification. The church is not a building, but a group of redeemed people (saints) who explain the good news about Jesus so we can believe in Christ and receive forgiveness of sins. These saints will feed and nurture us when we need knowledge, pray for us when we need help, encourage us when we lose heart, discipline us when we go astray, and bury our bodies when we die. When Christ returns to judge, he will raise our new and incorruptible bodies to eternal life with God, and we will be forever free from the penalty, power, and presence of sin.

God is the One Who is Three

We have reached a place where we must walk a razor's edge in thinking about God. All Christians have found the truths above to be difficult to reconcile. Many people, however, have considered them to be impossible to accept. In particular, they charge the Bible with a contradiction. Either God is one or God is three, but he cannot be both one and three. To many, the quandary seems hopeless, yet Christians who have gone before us have done the heavy lifting, and we can feast on the fruit of their labor.

This doctrine is so foundational that all of the major historical confessions give it a prominent place.[3] Feed on the pregnant prose of Article 1 from The Thirty-Nine Articles of Religion: "There is but one living and true God, everlasting, without body, parts, or passions; of infinite power, wisdom, and goodness; the maker and preserver of all things both visible and invisible. And in unity of this Godhead there be three Persons, of one substance, power, and eternity; the Father, the Son, and the Holy Ghost." This is the doctrine of the Trinity and the subject of the next chapter.

—————— Things to Know ——————

– What are the 3 chief articles of the Apostles' Creed?

3. One of the earliest creeds affirming the trinity is the Nicene Creed, adopted in AD 325 and accepted by the Eastern Orthodox Church, Roman Catholic Church, and the Protestant Church. All Protestant creeds and confessions affirm the Nicene Creed.

—— 11 ——

The Logic of God

If Christ is God and God is God, are there not two Gods?

−BART EHRMAN, PROFESSOR OF RELIGIOUS STUDIES,
UNIVERSITY OF NORTH CAROLINA[1]

In the unity of the Godhead there be three persons, of one substance, power,
and eternity; God the Father, God the Son, and God the Holy Ghost: the Father
is of none, neither begotten, nor proceeding; the Son is eternally begotten of
the Father; the Holy Ghost eternally proceeding from the Father and Son.

−WESTMINSTER CONFESSION OF FAITH, 1647[2]

FEW PEOPLE HAVE HELD greater evangelical credentials than Bart Ehrman.
As a graduate of Moody Bible Institute and Wheaton College, two evangelical flagship schools, he appeared to be rising through the ranks of
evangelical Christianity. His journey changed dramatically, though, from
professing evangelical Christian leader to agnostic university professor because, he says, of the problem of suffering. His doubts about the Christian
faith emerged when he could not reconcile the existence of a loving God
with the existence of pain in the world.

Those doubts were reinforced as he studied the process by which we
got our present Bibles. He became convinced that the Bible was full of dis-
crepancies and contradictions. Those two issues, the problem of suffering
and the integrity of Scripture, are beyond the scope of this book. However,
the fact that I do not respond to them does not mean there is no substan-
tive response.[3] I am frankly surprised by the things that so easily shattered

1. Ehrman, *Jesus, Interrupted*, 254.

2. 2:3.

3. Randy Alcorn dedicates a chapter of his book on suffering to Bart Ehrman. See *If*

Ehrman's fragile faith, since these issues have been successfully confronted by intellectually sturdy Christians for centuries.

However, Ehrman does raise a point that is germane to this chapter. He insists that "important doctrines like the divinity of Christ and the doctrine of the Trinity . . . weren't the original teachings of Christianity . . ."[4] Granted, the Apostles' Creed was not formed in the apostles' lifetime, but I have labored to show how the Apostles' Creed is an accurate summary of the earliest Christian documents in existence, the New Testament. If Bart Ehrman can produce pertinent documents that are earlier than the New Testament documents, he has inexplicably failed to do so.

Of course, he is not alone in viewing doctrines like the Trinity as not only a later invention by the church, but logically unreasonable.

How the Trinity Is Like Gravity

Many skeptics have noted that the word "trinity" is not found in the Bible. That is true. The Bible, however, is replete with descriptions of God, and these descriptions can only be harmonized by the doctrine of the trinity. For Bart Ehrman or anyone else to make the claim that the doctrine of the trinity is not found in Scripture[5] is like saying the law of gravity is not found in science. From the beginning of history, humans have observed that some invisible force holds us to the earth. Later on, humans observed that the same force compels the planets to revolve around the sun. We all take these things for granted, and most of us don't spend much time thinking about them. Some people do, though, and in 1686 Isaac Newton went public with his "law of universal gravitation."

Although Einstein's theory of general relativity eventually superseded it, Newton's law, I am told, remains an excellent approximation of the effects of gravity. I am certainly no expert on Newtonian physics or Einstein's theories, but I know enough to know this. Gravity existed and could be described long before it was accurately captured in a formal statement of theory or law or even called "gravity." Similarly, the reality of the trinity existed and could be described long before it was accurately captured in a formal statement[6] of doctrine or even called "trinity." Just as there is

God is Good, 95.

4. Morgan, "Complete Interview with Bart Ehrman."

5. Ehrman, *Jesus, Interrupted*, 260.

6. Such as the Nicene Creed which was adopted by the Council of Nicaea in AD 325.

progressive understanding in the discipline of science, there is progressive understanding in the discipline of theology. The truth doesn't change, or contradict previous truth, but our understanding of the truth can become clearer. In the Bible, we have an accurate record of God describing himself. In the doctrine of the trinity, we have a sensible harmonization of that data.

The Four Reconcilable Facts of the Doctrine of the Trinity

While the word *trinity* is not found in the Bible, the doctrine that the word represents is the only reasonable way to reconcile all the data given in Scripture. Here are four facts we have to deal with:

> There is one God.
>
> The Father is God.
>
> The Son is God.
>
> The Holy Spirit is God.

At every place, the Bible assumes these facts to be true. If you look carefully, you will see them everywhere. For example, in Matthew 28:19, Jesus tells his disciples to baptize new believers "in the name of the Father and of the Son and of the Holy Spirit." Did God inspire bad grammar? Why is "name" singular? Since there are three persons, shouldn't Jesus say "in the *names* of the Father and of the Son and of the Holy Spirit?" No, the words are chosen carefully. There is only one God and he exists as three persons.

In chapter two we mentioned the importance of reason in interpreting Scripture. Someone might protest at this point and say that these statements represent a contradiction that looks like this:

> There is one God (A)
>
> There is not one God (non-A)

I agree that this is a contradiction, but I disagree that this is the doctrine of the trinity. Rather, the doctrine of the trinity looks like this:

> There is one God (A)
>
> God is three persons (B)

There is no logical contradiction, but there is a good bit of mystery. There are some things that we all believe even if we don't understand them. That is not fluffy religious-speak. Even in the hard sciences, experts believe many things to be true that they do not understand. They have collected a good bit of data but have yet to settle on a unified theory of everything. If there were still no mysteries in our universe, there would be no need for scientists. Scientists believe what they don't understand every day. God is a being who exists as three persons, and you have trouble wrapping your mind around that because there is nothing in your experience quite like it.

How the Trinity is Like a Cell Phone

When you want to explain or understand any new concept, the first thing you do is relate the unknown to the known. Imagine visiting a stone-age tribe at the Equator and trying to explain ice. Where would you begin?

Or imagine you can travel back in time and suddenly you are in the presence of Benjamin Franklin and Thomas Jefferson as they are editing an early draft of the Declaration of Independence. At one point they want to consult with John Adams on the wording of a particular phrase, but he is not present. "I wish I had my cell phone," you say, "I'd just call him." "What is a cell phone?" asks the ever-curious Franklin. Now how do you begin to answer? "It's an electronic hand-held device," you respond, "and when I talk into it I can have a conversation with anyone just about anywhere in the world."

They stare blankly, so you continue. "A cell phone," you explain, "is like a hybrid between a landline phone and a two-way radio." What are you doing? You are trying to relate the unknown to the known, but landlines and two-way radios are unknowns to Jefferson and Franklin. They are brilliant men, but they still cannot understand you. "Illogical!" says Franklin. "Unreasonable!" snorts Jefferson. Actually, there is nothing at all illogical or unreasonable about cell phones, but in the eighteenth century, it might have seemed so.[7] Had they lived another two centuries, both men would have increased in their knowledge and more easily grasped the concept of a cell phone. Such is our understanding of the doctrine of the trinity. When we think correctly about God, we have to conclude that in this doctrine there is no infraction of the laws of logic. In the future, our understanding will grow and our thinking about God will become clearer.

---

7. I first used this illustration in my book *Which 'Real' Jesus?*, 55–56.

Bart Ehrman remains steadfast in his rejection of the doctrine of the Trinity. That is because he continues to reject the reliability and authority of Scripture. Those doubts began with his inability to reconcile the existence of a sovereign and good God with the suffering and evil in the world. He is not the first to wrestle with these issues, and he will not be the last to be overcome by them. There are answers to these questions for those who want them. The answers do not come easily, because thinking about God has always required some vigorous intellectual exercise.

As Christians, we know our system of belief has some thorny problems, but we maintain that it has fewer problems than any other system. How, for example, will Bart Ehrman's agnosticism help him explain and cope with the problem of evil and suffering? The agnostic can only see suffering as random, pointless, and absurd, while the Christ-follower understands that suffering has not only a cause, but also a purpose, in the sovereign plan of God. It seems that Ehrman has traded one faith system with problems for another faith system with greater problems.

Only God knows the motives of the heart, but Scripture bears witness that the intellectual rejection of God is fundamentally a moral rebellion. We have a king, but we do not want him to rule. He has all authority, but we do not want to submit. He has given us his laws, but we do not want to obey. Those laws are the focus of the next chapter.

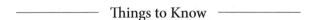

Things to Know

- What are the 4 reconcilable facts of the doctrine of the trinity?

—— 12 ——

Diets, Days, Dress, and Despair

As a kid, I was pushed into the Baptist church, taught that way. As an adult, I was able to seek out information on my own to find out that the Muslim religion, Rastafari, Baptist, Christian—that they all the same . . . They all God-fearing people and love is love . . . It's more based on life and a way of life and liberty as opposed to religion because religion is so false, because it's so past tense and written by someone who is not here. I feel like religion should be based on the way you live and the way you treat yourself and treat others.

—SNOOP DOGG, RAPPER, ENTERTAINER[1]

Beside this law, commonly called moral, God was pleased to give to the people of Israel, as a church under age, ceremonial laws, containing several typical ordinances, partly of worship, prefiguring Christ, his graces, actions, sufferings and benefits; and partly holding forth diverse instructions of moral duties. All which ceremonial laws are now abrogated under the New Testament . . . To them also, as a body politic, he gave sundry judicial laws, which expired together with the state of that people, not obliging any other now, further than the general equity thereof may require . . . the moral law doth for ever bind all.

—WESTMINSTER CONFESSION OF FAITH, 1647[2]

AS YOU READ THE Bible, you will soon discover that it contains a lot of rules. I don't deny it. The Bible is full of dos and don'ts. They go by various names like commandments, precepts, instruction, and statutes, but the most common name for all of these mandates is the law.

1. Pearson, "Q&A: Snoop Dogg on Criticism."
2. 19:3–5.

Already we have a problem in this anti-authoritarian age. This generation doesn't trust human institutions that make and enforce laws, and for
good reason. In our recent history these institutions have been discred-
ited by hypocrisy, corruption, and deception. The first lawmakers children
meet are their parents; then they are introduced to teachers, coaches, police
officers, presidents, senators, CEOs, even priests and pastors, who have
been entrusted with much power, but too often abuse it. In these social
institutions of family, education, business, religion, and government, there
have to be rules. Without rules there is chaos and the weak are exploited.
Imagine a busy intersection with no traffic signals, where everyone does
what they please. Tiny hybrid cars don't have a chance. In a world without traffic signals, I want to be in the armored Hummer! Too often the
rule-makers turn out to be hypocrites, placing themselves above the law.
Lawmakers are prone to make laws that are self-serving. And too often,
the rules themselves are burdensome, confusing, self-perpetuating, archaic,
ambiguous, manipulative, and tedious.

That's the way many people see the laws of the Bible. The laws found in
the Old Testament are especially confounding. They often speak of an agri-
cultural world that most modern people do not understand. And then there
are those pesky rules governing warfare that contain troublesome commands
to kill other human beings. So what is going on here? Theologians have long
noted that the Bible contains three kinds of law. Knowing these three categories of law will go a long way to understanding how to please God.

The Moral Law: Repeated in the New Testament

The moral law refers to a God-given absolute standard of right and wrong
that is timeless. The moral law is true and binding for every person in every
generation and in every culture. There is never a time or place in which the
moral law is not applicable. For the most part, the moral law is codified in
what we call the Ten Commandments. All of the Ten Commandments, except the command to keep the Sabbath, are repeated in the New Testament
by the apostles. These repeated commands are therefore binding on the
New Testament believer. For example, it has always been wrong to murder,
it is wrong now, and it will always be wrong.

The Ceremonial Law: Repealed in the New Testament

The ceremonial law refers to the temporary ceremonies and rituals that accompanied the worship of God by the nation of Israel. The purpose of these laws was to prepare God's people for their Messiah, who would deliver them from their enemies and save them from their sins. Think, for example, how the drama of Yom Kippur, the Day of Atonement or the Day of Covering, foreshadowed the future work of Jesus Christ. Once a year, two goats were brought before the High Priest. He placed his hands on each goat's head, symbolizing the transfer of sin and guilt from the people to these innocent substitutes. One goat was then sacrificed at the altar of the temple where the High Priest would collect a bowl of its blood. From there, he would take the blood into the Holy of Holies, where he would sprinkle the blood on the ark of the covenant which contained the Ten Commandments. Over the course of the previous year, the people had broken these commandments on a trillion or so occasions and they deserved the wrath of a holy God. The only thing that stood between them and perfect, awful justice was this covering of blood from an innocent sacrifice.

The other goat did not meet such a ritualized demise. Instead, he was released and escaped into the wilderness, a "scapegoat" symbolizing how God mercifully allowed their sins to be carried far away so they were not counted against them. In a matter of days or hours, this defenseless and domesticated creature would meet its unceremonious end, the victim of wild predators or harsh elements. Either way, the message is clear: the wages of sin is death, but God will provide a way to cover and remove our sins through the blood sacrifice of an innocent substitute.

All of these rituals and ceremonies pointed to the cross of Christ. The Passover celebration prepared God's people for the one who would be "the Lamb of God, who takes away the sin of the world!" (John 1:29). Circumcision reminded them that the coming King would be from Abraham's seed, a physical descendant of Abraham in whom "all the families of the earth shall be blessed" (Gen 12:3). Even the many rules and rituals about diet and dress, important for the overall physical health and hygiene of a nation traveling through the wilderness, taught important lessons. As the people of God, their obedience would set them apart as holy, different, and separate from the surrounding nations.

The Civil Law: Repealed in the New Testament

The civil law is a body of ordinances that are necessary for running the just and merciful government of a nation with borders. Those borders needed to be defended, and, like all borders, they were to be defended by the power of the sword. In the only legitimate theocracy that has ever existed, the mission of the "church" (God's covenant people) and the sword of the state are welded together. In addition to "common defense," this theocratic government was responsible to maintain "domestic tranquility." Consequently, there are numerous tort laws in the Old Testament designed to hold people responsible for the health and well-being of their neighbors. These are the natural social outcomes of loving your neighbor. If a man digs a pit, for example, and leaves it uncovered, he is being irresponsible and unloving. If his neighbor's donkey falls in the pit, he must make restitution for the donkey (Exod 21:33). Failure to do so would result in punishment by the theocratic government.

With the coming of Christ, the King, a new day dawned. The only God-ordained theocracy that had ever existed had fulfilled its purpose and was dissolved by God. "My kingdom is not of this world," he explained to Pilate, "If my kingdom were of this world, my servants would have been fighting, that I might not be delivered over to the Jews. But my kingdom is not from the world" (John 18:36).

Jesus is clear that the focus of God is now no longer on Israel, but on the whole world (Acts 1:8). He had created and blessed Israel so that they could bless all the nations of the earth (Gen 12). They were to be a "kingdom of priests," reconciling even the Gentiles to God. However, they largely failed in this and God raised up another "Israel," the Christ who would do what the nation of Israel could not do, becoming a "light for the Gentiles" and bringing "salvation to the ends of the earth" (Isa 49:6). National borders now fade away. Geographical, social, and cultural barriers are torn down. Now "there is neither Jew nor Greek, there is neither slave nor free, there is no male and female, for you are all one in Christ Jesus" (Gal 3:28).

The good news message of reconciliation will be defended and advanced by the power of Spirit-enabled persuasion and preaching (Isa 49:2), not the power of the sword. Through logic and reason and plain-speaking, the evidence for the claims of Christ must be presented to a skeptical world. Through good works and compassion for the poor and marginalized, the church earns credibility, and the right to be heard. And while Jesus never commanded his disciples to kill for his message, he did prepare them to die for it (Luke 9:23).

In the Old Testament, the gospel was something for people to come and hear in Jerusalem. In the New Testament, the gospel is something that people go and tell to the ends of the earth. The people of God will not be contained by geographical borders, and the reign of Christ is not limited by national boundaries. He will reign in the hearts of men and women "from every tribe and language and people and nation" (Rev 5:9), and every day his kingdom advances.

Now the sword of the state is in the hands of a multitude of governments. Yet even if these political leaders do not worship the true and living God, they are still his instruments to restrain evil in this world (Rom 13:4). Providentially, God often uses even those who deny him to protect the church and make a way for the spread of the gospel. Nations that deny religious liberty should be the object of our protest. With the coming of Christ, the sword of the state is to be both out of the hands of the church and off of its neck, as human governments are held responsible by God to uphold justice and show mercy. Government officials who deny basic civil rights and religious freedom, will be held accountable by God (Acts 12:23).

A Test Case: Leviticus 18 and 19

It is hard to overemphasize the importance of knowing the difference between these three kinds of law. There is no single text that distinguishes one from the other, and some people have dismissed the distinction as man-made. Students of the Bible, however, have observed that some Old Testament laws are repeated in the New Testament by the apostles (the moral law) and some laws are repealed (the civil and ceremonial laws). As you read the Old Testament, all three kinds are intermingled, often in the same text, like a plate of spaghetti. Lovers of the Bible will take the time and care to untangle them.

An example is Leviticus 18 and 19. In the often-heated debate concerning same-sex relationships, faithful Christians must respectfully and compassionately uphold the sexual ethics that are clearly stated in the Bible. For example, Leviticus 18:22 says: "You shall not lie with a male as with a woman; it is an abomination." This seems to be a clear prohibition of same-sex relationships, and an obvious clue that same-sex marriage is not pleasing to God.

Not so fast, says an opponent. In the very next chapter, men are told not to get haircuts or trim their beards (19:27). And God's covenant people must eat their peace offering sacrifice on the same day they kill the animal (19:5). These kinds of laws are the object of much ridicule by skeptics, and often used to discredit the Christian faith. Since Christians don't regard these laws as binding, they reason, how can they regard other laws in the same context as binding? This appears to be a case of Christians being conveniently inconsistent, but appearances can be deceiving.

When an unbelieving friend uses this argument with me, I ask him or her to look at the two commands surrounding the prohibition of same-sex relationships. The first command prohibits throwing your children into a fire to sacrifice them to pagan gods (18:21). The second commandment prohibits raping animals (18:23). I then ask, "Do you think these are good laws?" Of course they do (since most of them love babies who have been born and animals in general). What about the command prohibiting your neighbor from committing adultery with your wife? (18:20). Is that a good law? Most agree that these prohibitions are sensible, just, and loving.

So they are guilty of what they charge: being inconsistent. They are picking and choosing which laws are binding, but at least my method of picking and choosing is not arbitrary. Ceremonial laws about beards and blood sacrifices have been clearly repealed in the New Testament (Acts 10:13) by the apostles, while moral laws governing sexual intimacy have been repeated (Rom 1:27; 1 Cor 6:9; 1 Tim 1:10). In this, Christians are being perfectly consistent.

Knowing and Doing

At first, it might seem that it is now an easy thing to please God. Without those cumbersome Old Testament laws, we can simply focus on a few rules to live by, but even if we are successful in untangling the permanent moral law from the temporary ceremonial law, we still have a huge problem. None of us obey it. In this sense, even the moral law can lead us to despair. If you really think you can obey the moral law, that is because you have never carefully looked at what the moral law requires. In the next chapter we take the time to do just that.

──────── Things to Know ────────

- What are the 3 kinds of law?

—— 13 ——

The Big Ten

Many people find religion to be very inspiring. Myself, I found it very stifling. I grew up with Christianity and I remember questioning it greatly. Some things didn't work for me. Some things did . . . I got my issues. Man, you don't want to get me started.

—BRAD PITT, AMERICAN ACTOR AND FILM PRODUCER[1]

Q. 114: But can those who are converted to God keep these commandments perfectly? No, for even the holiest of them make only a small beginning in obedience in this life.

—HEIDELBERG CATECHISM, 1563

CHRISTIANS HAVE UNDERSTOOD THE moral law of God to be summarized in the Ten Commandments, which first appear as a list in Exodus 20. "What is the law of God?" asks Question 92 of the Heidelberg Catechism. The answer reports, "God spoke all of these words, saying," and what follows is a concise explanation of the Ten Commandments. In the next few pages, I follow that time-honored tradition of commenting on the Ten Commandments and commending them to my generation.

First Commandment: No Other Gods

The first commandment requires that we have "no other gods before" the Lord our God who brought the Hebrews "out of Egypt" (Exod 20:1). Specifically, this commandment forbids idolatry, putting a created thing above the Creator as an object of worship or devotion (Rom 1:25). Idolatry is

1. Marikar, "Brad Pitt and More."

placing our trust in anything or anyone other than God for all of our good. It is tempting to think that we break this commandment only if we choose another religion. Buddhists, Hindus, Animists, and Muslims are idolaters, but since I am a Christian, I must be immune, right? The reality is that Christians break this commandment daily.

We can make idols out of anything: people, possessions, pleasure, and positions of power. Idolatry is choosing to displease God in order to please others (Gal 1:10; Acts 5:29). Therefore, we can worship wives and husbands, boyfriends and girlfriends, bosses and employees, movie stars and rock stars, parents and even our own children. Idolatry is trusting in some created thing for our happiness in this life and the life to come. Therefore, we can trust in money and sex, cars and clothes, Harleys and hunting, beer and oxycodone, football and golf. Idolatry is seeking to manipulate others, including imagined deities, to serve, admire, and even worship us. Therefore we can place our faith in positions of power, the exalted status we achieve through academics, athletics, or the arts. The list of "other gods" is endless because our hearts are what John Calvin called "a perpetual factory of idols."[2] We break the first commandment any time we do not "flee from idolatry" (1 Cor 10:14), falling short of giving our full allegiance and heart-felt worship to the God who has revealed himself in the Bible.

Second Commandment: No Carved Images

The second commandment requires us to abstain from making for ourselves "a carved image, or any likeness of anything that is in heaven above, or that is in the earth beneath, or that is in the water under the earth" (Exod 20:4). Here we are prohibited from drawing or shaping with our own hands any object of worship. Specifically, the second commandment forbids us from drawing pictures or making statues of God. "No one has ever seen God" (John 1:18), so there is no possibility that God could ever be accurately represented by an artist. Any depiction would mislead us and communicate an inaccurate view of God. God has revealed himself to us in words, not pictures, likely because pictures are subject to such diverse interpretation.

Think about that for a minute. If you are a homeowner, you are in possession of a deed. That deed spells out in great detail exactly what you own. Would you rather have that deed, or a child's crayon drawing of your house given to you by the seller you bought it from? Imagine producing

2. Calvin, *Institutes*, 1:108.

that drawing when you are called on to prove your ownership in court. Legal documents are always word-based, not image-based, in order to clarify as much as is humanly possible, the truth of the matter. Nothing good can come of drawing or sculpting an icon of God.

What about the pictures of Jesus you may have seen on your grandmother's wall? Before you decide, consider few things. First, no artist knows what Jesus looked like and all artists are biased. Artists of European descent typically paint a European Jesus. American filmmakers usually choose a good-looking white guy to play the role of the Jewish Messiah who was physically unimpressive (Isa 53:2). Artists who want a docile, meek, soft Jesus tend to draw an effeminate, passive man to depict the hard-handed carpenter from Galilee. Without a word, a child's perception of Jesus can be forever shaped (or rather misshaped) by a picture on the wall or in a stained glass window.

Christians will disagree about these matters, but my wife and I decided our children would grow up in a house that had no artists' prejudiced renditions of the second person of the Trinity. I find wise counsel in the Heidelberg Catechism's Question 98: "But may not pictures be tolerated in churches as books for the laity?" Keep in mind that this catechism was written in an age of high adult illiteracy. Most laymen could not read and those who could had little access to the Scripture or books on theology. Some argued that instead of words, we should teach these uneducated people with pictures. The answer to question 98 comes back: "No; for we should not be wiser than God, who will not have his people taught by dumb idols, but by the lively preaching of his Word."

Third Commandment: Revere God's Name

When a teenager texts the letters "OMG," she is likely breaking the third commandment. God plainly tells us: "You shall not take the name of the Lord your God in vain, for the Lord will not hold him guiltless who takes his name in vain" (Exod 20:7). When we speak of God, we must not be careless, casual, or flippant. Jokes about God should be off limits. Careless references to God (e.g., "the man upstairs") should be avoided. Invoking God as your witness when you intend to lie (e.g., "so help me God"), breaking an oath, or using God's name as just one more exclamation when you are startled, are all violations of this command. Cursing others who offend you, angrily invoking God to damn them, or telling them to go to hell, will make you guilty of breaking this law.

Using God's name in an empty way, cheaply and without respect, violates the third commandment. When we sing our songs of praise to God on Sunday morning, in the company of believers in public worship, we often break this commandment. When we say in our songs how much we love God, obey God, praise God, adore God, exalt God, and will leave everything behind in order to follow God, we had better mean it. If these things are not truly the desires of our heart, to say them aloud, even in our singing, is to use the Lord's name in vain. Even calling ourselves "Christians," taking on the Lord's family name, can be dangerous. We must then live like Christians, "so that the name of God and the teaching may not be reviled" (1 Tim 6:1). Like all the moral laws, there are countless ways to break this command.

Fourth Commandment: Remember God's Day

In the Ten Commandments, the fourth commandment is a special case. "Remember the Sabbath day, to keep it holy. Six days you shall labor, and do all your work, but the seventh day is a Sabbath to the Lord your God. On it you shall not do any work" (Exod 20:8–10). God gave this gift to his people as one day in seven to rest from their work and to enjoy their friends, family, and the fruit of their labor. Here was a great opportunity to give leisurely time to contemplating his Word and communicating in prayer. Yet this is the only commandment of the ten that is not repeated in the New Testament.

In fact, the Sabbath, as the Jews knew it, seems to be considered a ceremonial law that was repealed in the New Testament (Col 2:16, 17; Rom 14:5). And yet, in the New Testament another day emerges as a special day of the week. This day was not a day of rest as much as it was a day of worship. On this day, the first day of the week, which we call Sunday, New Testament believers gathered for worship of the risen Lord. This day became significant because Jesus was raised on the first day of the week (Matt 28:1). He waited a week and appeared to them again, on a Sunday (John 20:19). From the earliest days, the apostles were planting churches that met together on the first day of the week, to worship, share in the Lord's Supper (Acts 20:7), and collect offerings for the Lord's work (1 Cor 16:2). So when the writer of Hebrews warns Christians to "not neglect to meet together"

(Heb 10:25), we assume that the most likely time of that meeting was on Sunday, in honor of the risen Lord.

Given this history, most Christians understand that there remains a special day in the week, one day out of seven, that is ordained for us to turn from our normal weekly activities and give unusual attention to God. The Sabbath of the Old Testament has become "the Lord's Day" (Rev 1:10) of the New Testament.

Fifth Commandment: Honor Your Parents

God intends for the treasure of his self-revelation, the Word of God, to be transferred from generation to generation, from parents to children (Deut 6:7). Fathers and mothers must speak God's truth, and sons and daughters must listen. So it is not surprising that the fifth commandment implores children to "honor your father and your mother" (Exod 20:12). If children refuse to honor their parents and choose to rebel, the transfer of truth will be tragically aborted.

"Children," writes the Apostle Paul, "obey your parents in the Lord, for this is right. Honor your father and mother (this is the first commandment with a promise), that it may go well with you and that you may live long in the land" (Eph 6:1–3). Special blessings await boys and girls who humbly submit to the wise counsel of godly parents. Untold misery and unmeasured grief can be avoided when children honor parents who honor the Lord. One book of the Bible in particular, Proverbs, makes this truth its theme. "Hear, my son, your father's instruction, and forsake not your mother's teaching" (Prov 1:8).

In our younger years, while we are financially dependent, physically weak, and intellectually undeveloped, we show honor by listening carefully to our parents, telling them the truth, and obeying their commands. In this, we humbly acknowledge that our parents know more than we do about the most important things in life. In our later years, when we have become financially independent, physically stronger, and emotionally mature, we are responsible to honor our parents by seeking their advice, valuing their opinions, and insuring that their basic physical needs are met as they grow weaker. As they cared for us in our youth, we care for them in their old age. The failure of Christians to honor their parents in this way discredits the gospel (1 Tim 5:8).

The essence of the fifth commandment is that God has put in place an authority structure on this earth through which he governs the relationships that people have with God and each other. The first authority figures a child will know are parents. Next come pastors, elders, teachers, coaches, police officers, mall security guards, employers, drill instructors, judges, and governors. If a young child does not learn his proper place by honorably relating to parents, he or she will find all of life to be unnecessarily difficult.

If God has entrusted children to your care, you are responsible to teach them to respect you and their mother, and by extension to respect other authority figures in their lives. They will learn a great deal by watching you relate to their grandparents.

Honoring your own parents can be challenging, but as your skills in handling the Bible grow, you will learn how to address the many questions that are raised by this command: What if my parents are not Christians? What if they do not give godly counsel? What if they command me to disobey God? What if they abused me? What if they are divorced? What if they waste money I give them? Once again, the Word of God is sufficient to guide you to a wise course of action in each individual case. In the Word, you will find that all human authority has its limits, some authorities should be challenged, even disobeyed, and irresponsible parents should not be enabled. The bottom line is that the way you speak to, speak about, listen to, and care for your parents should be marked by biblically-informed honor, even when they do not deserve it.

Sixth Commandment: No Murder

The sixth commandment is terse: "You shall not murder" (Exod 20:13). It seems clear enough, but it requires some explanation. The Hebrew word for murder is not the same as the Hebrew word for "kill." In times of war or self-defense or capital crimes, historic Christianity has argued that Christians might be authorized to take a human life. There is, writes Solomon, "a time to kill" (Eccl 3:3), but there is never a time to murder.

What is murder? Murder is taking our own life or the life of another that we are not authorized by God to take. The first murder in human history was motivated by jealousy and fueled by anger (Gen 4:6–8). As in the first murder, most murders are committed against someone the murderer knows. The murderer wants what another person has, whether it is money, popularity, parental approval, or the love of a woman. Jealousy stirs up anger and anger unchecked seeks the destruction of its object (James 4:1–2). The destruction usually begins with a verbal assault, using words as weapons to inflict pain. Hatred, though, is not easily satisfied, and angry words often lead to violent confrontation. In the case of Cain, when he found himself alone with Abel in the field, he "rose up against his brother Abel and killed him" (Gen 4:8).

So the sixth commandment not only condemns the violent act of murdering a human being. It also condemns the corruption of the human heart that conceives and carries out the homicide. Most people give a cursory glance to the Ten Commandments and grant themselves a passing grade. The vast majority of us will make it through our whole lives without committing unjustified homicide. That does not mean we have kept the sixth commandment. Jesus acknowledges that the sixth commandment does indeed prohibit the physical act of murder, but beyond that "I say to you that everyone who is angry with his brother will be liable to judgment; whoever insults his brother will be liable to the council; and whoever says, 'You fool!' will be liable to the hell of fire" (Matt 5:22). Of course, no one meets this standard, and that is precisely the point Jesus is trying to make.

The implications are stunning. The sixth commandment comes to bear on a vast array of relevant issues like suicide, physician-assisted suicide, abortion, end-of-life decisions, physical fitness, smoking, under-exercising, overeating, overdrinking, bullying, name-calling, and the tone of discourse in political debates.

Seventh Commandment: No Adultery

No human relationship takes priority over marriage. A man is expected to "leave his father and his mother and hold fast to his wife" (Gen 2:24), but he should never leave his wife. Husband and wife are united in a way that stabilizes society and symbolizes God's relationship with us. In our marriage vows we make public promises, surrounded by a wedding party made up of our closest friends. The role of these friends is to bear witness to our vows, and then, if they are true friends, hold us accountable to our solemn oath for the rest of our lives. Our God is a vow-keeping God and we, his ambassadors, must be a vow-keeping people.

Marriage tests a man's character like nothing else. Here he is called on to keep promises even when it is difficult, love even when it is not returned, forgive when offended, protect when it is dangerous, and provide even if it is not appreciated. In other words, he is to be godly. These are the kinds of things God does for us, and he expects us to follow his example.

Marriage is not something we do. It is something God does. "What therefore God has joined together," said Jesus, "let not man separate" (Matt 19:6). Since you didn't put it together, Jesus is saying, it is not your place to take it apart. In marriage, two people become "one flesh" (Matt 19:6). The oneness of a Christian marriage occurs at three levels. Husband and wife are joined spiritually, sharing the same life mission of glorifying God and enjoying him forever. They are joined emotionally, creating the safest of all environments in the home, bearing one another's burdens, comforting each other in sorrow, rejoicing in one another's joy, crying and laughing together. And they are joined sexually, allowed, even commanded, to experience sexual pleasure with one another (Prov 5:18; see also 1 Cor 7:5; Heb 13:4).

Marriage is fundamentally built on trust. Adultery is fundamentally built on lies. Show me an adulterer and I'll show you a liar. An affair is a logistical nightmare, requiring lies for the set up and the cover up. Nothing shreds a man's reputation as violently and efficiently as marital infidelity. If he can lie to his wife, he really can lie to anyone.

In addition to adultery, sexual immorality also belittles marriage (Heb 13:4). Previous generations called this fornication, and it covers a broad range of sexual sin, including sex between unmarried people. So, sex before marriage is another way to dishonor marriage. Another abuse of sex that falls under sexual immorality is genital intimacy with members of the same sex. The Bible uniformly condemns these practices outright as we have already seen. This prohibition is implied in the very definition of marriage that Jesus gives us: "a man shall leave his father and his mother and hold fast to his wife" (Matt 19:5). Marriage is a covenant that binds one man to one woman, and sex is not permitted outside of marriage. Therefore, sex with members of the same sex is off limits.

So the seventh commandment prohibits sex outside of marriage, sex before marriage, and sex with members of the same sex. Just in case there is any adult left on the planet who thinks he or she has not violated the seventh commandment, Jesus offers this insight: "But I say to you that everyone who looks at a woman with lustful intent has already committed adultery with her in his heart" (Matt 5:28). Cultivating thoughts about sex outside of marriage, sex before marriage, and sex with members of the same sex is also a violation of the seventh commandment. Every generation has struggled with this temptation, but it has probably never been more difficult to do the right thing. Long before internet pornography, C.S. Lewis warned that "there are people who want to keep our sex instinct inflamed in order to make money out of us."[3] Nearly a half-century later, almost everywhere a man turns today, he is assaulted with images that provoke lust.

So the larger intent of the seventh commandment is to guard the institution of marriage and help others guard it. For that reason, Christians should be careful in how they talk about sex (Eph 5:3, 4), modest in how they dress (1 Tim 2:9), vigilant in the company they keep (1 Cor 15:33), and cautious in their social interaction with members of the opposite sex (2 Sam 11:3). In short, followers of Christ should generally avoid the circumstances where it would be easy to sin sexually (1 Cor 6:18; 2 Tim 2:22; Gen 39:12). Married Christians should cultivate the conditions for a satisfying sex life, and, given the realities of ever-present sexual temptation, most single Christians should not delay marriage too long.

While these restrictions on sexual freedom seem harsh to most people today, keep in mind that they come from a loving God. Sex is the most powerful expression of human intimacy. To be naked, with literally nothing between you and another person, is to be vulnerable in the extreme. What should be an expression of selfless love is often a weapon of selfish exploitation. Emotions are toyed with, people are manipulated, jealousies are inflamed, and trust is destroyed. Nothing damages and scars the human soul quite like sex misused. In love, God regulates and restricts his gift, not for our detriment, but for our good.

Eighth Commandment: No Stealing

There are a million ways to take what is not yours. Armed robbery is obvious, but using your company's office supplies for personal use is not. Following from the seventh commandment above, to take the virginity of someone you have not married is to take what does not belong to you, but our culture never thinks of sexual immorality as stealing. When a student cheats on a test, he is stealing answers that are not his. When you share your all-you-can-eat salad with those at your table, you are committing "theft by buffet."

To steal is to insult another human being, saying in essence, "I am more important than you. My needs are greater. My pleasure takes priority over yours." It is contrary to loving others as yourself and doing to others what you want them to do to you.

3. Lewis, *Mere Christianity*, 92.

We can steal by not giving a customer, client, patient, or employer what they pay for. Through shoddy work or laziness or exaggerating billable hours or browsing the Internet on company time, we deprive another of what is rightfully theirs. We can steal by being delinquent on our accounts payable, delaying by 30 or 60 or 90 days what should have been paid on time.

Then there are the many ways we can rob God (Mal 3:8). God owns it all and "the earth is the Lord's" (1 Cor 10:26). He entrusts his money and goods to us, and he wants us to enjoy these gifts for ourselves. He also wants us to share with others, especially the poor, and invest in eternity by supporting our church's evangelistic and missions efforts (1 Tim 6:3–19; 2 Cor 8–9; Phil 1:5). He does not give us money and possessions to spend only on ourselves, cluttering our lives with gadgets and gizmos and the latest hi-tech toys. By not giving generously and sacrificially to the Lord's work and workers, supporting his church, we steal from God much as an embezzling employee, taking money out of circulation that should be advancing his enterprise.

We steal by living a life of excess and luxury while billions of people have yet to hear the gospel even once. We steal by not living within our means, amassing consumer debt, and paying interest that should be invested in eternity. We steal by refusing to work while expecting assistance from friends, family, church, or the government (2 Thess 3:10).

We steal by failing to manage our money well, wasting enormous sums over the years because of poor planning. We steal through filing or soliciting frivolous lawsuits, aiming to hit the jackpot. We steal by not honoring contracts or exploiting workers by not paying them a fair salary. We steal by tolerating regressive tax codes. We steal by wasting God's money in casinos and on lottery tickets, lured by easy money. There are a million ways to break the eighth commandment.

Most importantly, stealing is an egregious insult to God. It is a bald and blatant statement to the world that we do not believe God provides for our needs. When we do not believe God is good enough, wise enough, and strong enough to take care of us, we take matters into our own hands and steal from others.

Ninth Commandment: No Lying

Lies are the accomplices of all law-breaking. When we worship other gods, it is because we have believed lies about the true God. The most common way to dishonor parents is to lie to them. When a man commits adultery, he has to lie to his wife, and he often recruits others to lie for him. Likewise, stealing normally gets an assist from deception. And then, when evil-doers are brought to justice, justice can be miscarried through a lying witness. Think how many other sins could be prevented if this one command was always obeyed. What kind of world this would be if everyone always and only spoke the truth in love (Eph 4:15) or didn't speak at all?

The most obvious prohibition in this law is perjury. To bear false witness destroys the integrity of the court. By lies, the power of the court can be manipulated for personal gain, used to extort, steal, and murder. Without the truth, judges cannot give proper verdicts, and laws are not enforced. Un-enforced laws lead to anarchy, innocent people suffer, and civilized culture disintegrates. When citizens lose confidence in the courts, society begins to unravel. Like all of these commands, there are count-less applications of the command "You shall not bear false witness against your neighbor" (Exod 20:16).

We can also bear false witness against our neighbor outside of court. By outright slander we murder his reputation. By gossip we pass on or re-ceive damaging information without checking the facts. By failing to speak up and defend another's reputation when we know the facts exonerate him, we diminish him in the eyes of others with our silence. We break the ninth commandment by making promises or contracts we don't intend to keep, or not keeping promises or contracts we originally thought we would keep, but proved to be difficult (Ps 15:4). By speaking half-truths, we mislead others. By flattery, we manipulate others. By boasting, we deceive others by exalting our strengths and hiding our weaknesses in self-worship.

There are two main motives for lying. First, we lie to gain some plea-sure. In the pursuit of pleasure, teenage boys tell girls they love them in order to get sex, CFOs cook the books in order to make a company look profitable to stockholders, alcoholics tell their loved ones they have not been drinking, employees inflate the numbers on their expense account, pastors exaggerate the size of their church, and politicians distort their op-ponents' voting record in attack ads. Second, we lie to escape pain. In trying to escape pain, children insist they did not get into the cookies before din-ner, political figures guilty of extra-marital affairs look into the camera and deny everything, and murderers plead "not guilty." None of these things are expressions of love to others. Lying is fundamentally a selfish act.

And then there is blasphemy, which is to lie about God. When we teach, or preach, or say things about God that are not true, we break the ninth commandment. When we misquote or misrepresent God because we have been sloppy in our study and careless in our doctrine, we lie to others about what God is like (2 Tim 2:15; Gal 1:7; 2 Cor 4:2).

Lying is not only selfish, but foolish. Lies beget lies until the liar himself believes them. It seems like a quick fix at the time, but lies eventually catch up with you. Not one lie will go unnoticed by God. And ultimately, since all of our lies to others are in the presence of God, we are lying to God himself.

When Ananias tried to give the impression to the church he was more generous than he actually was, Peter gave him the bad news: "You have not lied to men, but to God." Under severe discipline, Ananias then "fell down and died" (Acts 5:4–5). By grace, God does not discipline all of us in the same manner. Who could survive? Who among us has not lied to our church family, giving the impression we are more godly, more holy, more generous, more committed to Jesus than we really are? Some church members lie so long about the state of their spiritual lives that they become comfortable with the sorry façade, maintaining the mask for decades until the day they die. Everybody lies.

Tenth Commandment: No Coveting

In the unlikely event that you arrived at this point thinking you have kept God's moral law, brace yourself. When God says, "You shall not covet," he is saying that you should be so content with what he has provided you that you will not seek to satisfy yourself outside of his will (Heb 13:5). You will not become jealous or envious of others who have what you don't. You will not take measures to get what they have or otherwise separate them from it, whether it is their wife, their star employee, their car, or their good reputation. You will in fact, find pleasure in the pleasure they take in what God has given them. Surely this is what it means to love them as you love yourself.

This does not mean we cannot seek to improve our own situation. When you are discontent with your present job, it is not necessarily wrong to seek another one that is better, but it is wrong to be ungrateful for the job you have now. At least you have a job. It is also wrong to seek a job in a way that does harm to another person. Participating in office politics, forming self-serving alliances, engaging in strategic flattery, and slandering those who are competing for the same position are all the rotten fruit of coveting.

We break this commandment when our discontent leads us to complain and whine and bellyache about how little we have and how much we want. We break the tenth commandment when we fail to be grateful and give thanks to God for all the good things he has given us. We break the tenth commandment when we rejoice in our neighbor's loss and mourn our neighbor's success, even our competitors in sports and business. As you can see, coveting is at the root of most other sins. Why do we lie and lust and kill and steal? We love ourselves, we want what someone else has, and we want it now.

How Are You Doing So Far?

By now something should be painfully clear. The title of this chapter could be misunderstood. If the way to please God is by obeying his law, then we can't please God. Because the standard is so unspeakably high, there is no hope for any of us. None of us has kept the law, and if we come into right relationship by keeping the law, the law is something I hate. It represents a barrier not a bridge. It reminds me of my dismal failure and mocks my weak efforts. Even if we think we have kept a large portion of the law, it is not good enough. James declares that "whoever keeps the whole law but fails in one point has become accountable for all of it" (Jas 2:10). Paul reminds us that "no one is justified before God by the law" (Gal 3:11). This truth led the authors of the Heidelberg Catechism to write of the law:

> Question 5. Canst thou keep all these things perfectly?
>
> Answer: In no wise, for I am prone by nature to hate God and my neighbor.

The law in itself is not the good news. It is the worst possible news. There is a lawgiving God who demands perfect obedience and none of us will ever come close to meeting the law's demands. Because the law condemns us, we stand guilty before a Holy God. God owes us nothing except the death penalty (Rom 6:23). For our crimes, we deserve to die and be in hell, eternally separated from his love and grace. What is the remedy?

─────── Things to Know ───────

– What are the 10 Commandments?

14

An Abuser's Guide to the Law

But, you know, when we think about our faith, the thing at root that we think about is, not only Christ sacrificing himself on our behalf, but it's also the Golden Rule, you know, treat others the way you would want to be treated.

−BARAK OBAMA, PRESIDENT OF THE UNITED STATES,
EXPLAINING HIS ENDORSEMENT OF SAME-SEX MARRIAGE[1]

Q:115: Why, then, does God have the ten commandments preached so strictly since no one can keep them in this life? First, that all our life long we may become increasingly aware of our sinfulness, and therefore more eagerly seek forgiveness of sins and righteousness in Christ. Second, that we may constantly and diligently pray to God for the grace of the Holy Spirit, so that more and more we may be renewed in the image of God . . .

−THE HEIDELBERG CATECHISM, 1563

THE APOSTLE PAUL TOLD Timothy "the law is good, if one uses it lawfully" (1 Tim 1:8). Which means it is possible to use the law unlawfully, in a way God never intended. In fact, the law of God can be abused in at least three ways.

Pragmatism: Using Law to Get the American Dream

There is great wisdom in the law of God, and those who follow it are wise. From the beginning, people and cultures that follow these laws have found that they generally lead to greater peace and prosperity, health, and wealth. Obedience to these laws has a stabilizing effect on society. Imagine a world where everyone loved their neighbor as themselves. Spouses, families, and

1. Calmes, "Obama Says."

neighbors would dwell in harmony, work hard, and look out for each other. The wealthy would voluntarily share their private property with the poor in ways that provide the poor with good jobs. People would be more thankful and content with what they have and avoid crippling debt. War, crime, poverty, illegitimacy, divorce, AIDS, racism, and abortion would end. Social justice would expand while the federal government and taxes would shrink. There would be no need for government intrusion to coerce justice. The rising tide would lift all boats, and all would prosper. But these gifts of prosperity can often eclipse the Giver, and focus turns away from the first four commandments to the last six as people want to hear more about "successful relationships" and "financial freedom."

Often churchgoers show up on Sunday to hear some good advice rather than the good news.[2] They are amused by "how-to" sermons that will lay out clear steps to financial security, physical healing, marital harmony, parental success, addiction recovery, and emotional bliss. There is nothing wrong in desiring these things, but when the law of God is reduced to formulas for personal happiness, something has gone awry. Christianity becomes just one more technique in a self-help world and loses its distinctive marks. Comedian Jon Stewart, host of Comedy Central's *The Daily Show*, sees through this abuse of the law when he says: "Religion makes sense to me. I have trouble with dogma more than I have trouble with religion . . . When people say things like, 'I found God and that helped me stop drinking,' I say, 'Great! More power to you. Just know that some people stop drinking without it.'"[3]

After all, millions have found similar help from Buddha, Muhammad, and Oprah to live better lives, pad their bank account, elevate their moods, kick their habits, and generally establish their idea of heaven on earth without the God of heaven. Most religions advocate various forms of the moral law and the ethic of love, but preachers who treat the Bible as a manual for personal improvement give non-Christians one more excuse to summarily dismiss the claims of Christ. Non-Christians are happy if your Bible works for you, but they have found something that works for them. That is the utilitarian essence of pragmatism: if it works for you, it is true for you. Likewise, if my method, technique, or belief system works for me, then it is true for me.

2. Horton, *Gospel-Driven Life*, 131–32.

3. Wallis, "The Truth Smirks."

In the end, many professing Christians make idols out of the gifts of God, seeing God as a powerful force to be harnessed and manipulated for their own pleasure and prosperity, serving their personal agenda. By keeping the laws of God, many hope to obligate God to reward them with what the rest of the world worships: health and wealth.

Legalism: Using the Law to Earn Heaven

The default religion of the world is legalism. This is the idea that we can earn God's love and favor by keeping his laws. New York Mayor Michael Bloomberg once boldly proclaimed, "I am telling you if there is a God, I'm not stopping to be interviewed. I am heading straight in. I've earned my place in heaven. It's not even close."[4] Why? Because he used his political influence to get people to stop smoking, lose weight, and say no to gun ownership.[5] Perhaps Mayor Bloomberg feels that this falls under God's command to love your neighbor.

In legalism, we try to obligate God to forgive our sins, and put him in a position of owing us heaven. Think about this for a minute: when was the last time a police officer pulled you over for driving the speed limit and gave you a cash reward on the spot? The police officer owes you nothing for obeying the law. Rather, you owe it to him and the rest of us to obey the law. When you obey, you are just doing your duty. Likewise, when we actually obey the law of God, we are only giving to God what we owe him. He is the Creator and we are his creatures; therefore, he owns us by right of creation. The Maker is the owner, and we owe him our obedience. In obeying the law, we merely give him his due.

He is a perfect Creator and he requires a perfect obedience. "For whoever keeps the whole law," writes James, "but fails in one point has become accountable for all of it" (Jas 2:10). Consider the case of two prisoners. One man is in prison for killing another man. The other man is in prison for killing ten men. Which one is the murderer? Both, of course. Likewise, you may know other people who have broken God's laws more frequently and egregiously than you have. Which one of you is the lawbreaker?

No sensible person would claim to be morally perfect. We all know we have failed to perfectly obey God's law, but our pride makes us hold tightly to our legalism. We begin to reason that since we have broken God's law at

4. Chumley, "Michael Bloomberg."
5. Chumley, "Michael Bloomberg."

several points, we can make it up to him by obeying him even more at others. In effect, we create a system to pay God back. World religions are structured on this premise. If you have done bad things, then do more good things in order to cancel it out. Accumulate good karma for the next life. Sure, you've incurred a debt, but if you work hard enough, you can pay God off.

Suppose again that a police officer pulls you over for speeding. He clocked you at 50 miles an hour in a 30-mile-an-hour zone. As he pulls out his pad to write the ticket, you begin to negotiate. "I'll make you a deal," you say. "I was over the speed limit for about 2 miles. Why don't I just drive the next two miles at 10 miles an hour and we'll call it even?" You can imagine the response. Yet every day, billions of people try to negotiate with God in similar ways. They think they can cancel out their law breaking by just doing more law keeping and self-depriving. They may observe special hours of prayer, submit to religious rituals, give to the poor, adopt an orphan, or go to church thinking this is payback that will get them into heaven. That's why so many are appalled when confronted by the truth: "Cursed be everyone who does not abide by all things written in the Book of the Law, and do them" (Gal 3:10). *All* things!

We owe a perfect God our perfect obedience to his perfect law. As law-breakers, God owes us nothing except his wrath, judgment, and hell. Everyone who tries to abuse the law by employing it as a means to earn a place in heaven will fail.

Relativism: Using the Law to Exalt Myself

Since it is obvious that none of us can keep the law perfectly, we tend to interpret the standards of the law relative to our ability to keep it. In other words, human beings are universally optimistic that God will grade us on a curve.

A few years ago, my son began competing in triathlons. After observing a few races, I decided I could get into shape and compete in my age group. In one of my first races, the race directors sent a group of physically disabled competitors first. Then they released the rest of us in order according to our estimated swim time. My son, who is much faster, started far ahead of me in the line. I made it through the swim, almost enjoyed the cycling portion, and nearly hit the wall in the run.

As I turned the corner and saw the finish line, I noticed one of the disabled racers just ahead of me. I deliberated for a moment, but my competitive juices were flowing and I couldn't resist. I kicked into high gear and began to notice the roar of the crowd. At first I thought they were trying to encourage me, but I quickly realized they were cheering for the very courageous man who was now beside me, and I regretted my decision to catch up to him. This was his moment, and I was in the way. But it was too late. I barely passed the man just a few feet in front of the finish line as hundreds of people took pictures of the man I just beat. My son, who had finished much earlier, came up to me and quipped, "Good job, Dad. Do you realize there are now going to be hundreds pictures on the Internet of you barely beating a man with one leg?"

We've laughed about that a lot since then, but that's the way most people cope with the law of God. Instead of comparing ourselves to perfection, we compare ourselves to other imperfect people; we are selective in our standards. In a race, you can almost always find someone slower and weaker than you are. When it comes to the law, you can always find people who break it more frequently and openly. Compared to them, you look pretty good.

Perhaps that's why we are fascinated with scandal. Where would the news media be if they could not report on people breaking the Ten Commandments? "If it bleeds, it leads," because they know that video of violent crime scenes grab our attention. Another politician gets caught in an affair and is forced to resign. Another child is abducted, molested, killed, and dumped in a field. Another terrorist blows up a marketplace. Another CEO gets caught in an elaborate and illegal financial scheme. Another sports celebrity buys a prostitute even though he has a supermodel wife at home. We love these stories, and we love to heap our disdain on the perpetrators largely because they make us look so much better. "I may not be perfect," we reason, "but at least I've never done that."

In terms of external conformity to the law in Jesus' day, it appeared that the Pharisees were in the elite class. They were religious professionals who kept the law for a living. Many of them were genuine and sincere people who loved God, but most of their leaders strongly opposed Jesus. He was horning in on their territory, and they saw him as a rival. Jesus warned his followers to beware of their teaching (Matt 16:12), so the Pharisees "went and plotted how to entangle him in his words" (Matt 22:15). They were meticulous in an outward show of external conformity, but they found all sorts of loopholes and double standards to let themselves off the hook. While they were careful to observe a host of religious rituals, they often neglected the broader demands of the law like "justice, mercy, and faithfulness" (Matt

23:23). This led Jesus to call them out: "You blind guides, straining out a gnat and swallowing a camel!" (Matt 23:24).

Jesus' criticism had a profound impact on the people listening to the debate. Most of the people looked to the Pharisees as the standard. If anyone had kept the law, the Pharisees certainly did. If anyone can be justified in God's sight by law-keeping, it must be the Pharisees. Yet Jesus blows these notions away with a single breath when he told the people that "unless your righteousness exceeds that of the scribes and Pharisees, you will never enter the kingdom of heaven" (Matt 5:20). Exceeds! Not just equals! If the Pharisees aren't good enough, then who is? What hope do we have if they have no hope? Jesus is pointing out that the Pharisees have abused the law through relativism, comparing themselves with people rather than with perfection and that led to an ugly pride.

The Ethic of Mutual Consent

Jesus' criticism has led some to conclude that Jesus doesn't really care much about specific laws as long as we focus on "justice and mercy and faithfulness" (Matt 23:23). But who determines what is just and merciful? Well, each of us has to decide that for ourselves, they argue, but the key is mutual consent. As long as no one gets hurt and the people involved are voluntary participants, it is ethical. At this point, the Golden Rule is liberally thrown about: "So whatever you wish that others would do to you, do also to them" (Matt 7:12). That sounds good, but our hearts are deceptive, and we have an unlimited ability to rationalize all sorts of behavior. A prostitute and her customer may possess a mutual consent, but that doesn't mean their night in a motel room is moral.

When I was a youth pastor in the 1980s in Houston, Texas, and the AIDs scare was widespread, I received many invitations from public schools to speak on abstinence as a viable option. I often began my talks by asking classes full of high school students for their best reasons for having sex before marriage. There are reasons behind everything we do, and I wanted to know their reasons for engaging in premarital sex. I told them I would write them on the board and we would discuss them. The best, strongest, most plausible reasons for having sex before marriage they could offer went something like this:

It's fun.

Everyone else is doing it.

It's good exercise.

To prove you're not gay.

To keep a boyfriend interested in you.

And then, without fail, someone would say, "Because you love each other." I spoke to thousands of students in those years and every single time, in every class, the person who offered this reason was a girl. I would ask her, "How do you know he loves you?" And she would say something like, "He told me so." Several studies on teenage sexuality during that time (as well as common sense) confirmed that most teenage boys were quite willing to lie to a girl, telling her he loved her, in order to get sex out of her.[6] I advised the girls that they will never really know for sure if a boy loves a girl until he is willing to promise, before witnesses, in a solemn and legally binding ceremony, that he will be faithful to her until death. Until then, he's just talking.

Notice how the Golden Rule is insufficient if it stands alone. The boys were usually silent at this point, but I can imagine one of them trying to defend his lust by saying, "I was just doing unto her as I wanted her to do unto me!" This is the same reasoning underneath consensual ethics. That is, many people, even professing Christians, believe that anything is moral as long it involves "consenting adults." Therefore, if a prostitute consents and her customer consents, their hour in a hotel is ethical. Or if two men consent to have sex, it is acceptable. Or if one man and two women consent to be married, it should be legal. By relativizing the law so that we determine what is right and wrong by what we want done to us, we unhitch it from the wisdom of the Creator, and give ourselves a god-like authority to follow our appetites.

One of the problems with consensual ethics is the reality of unforeseen and unintended consequences. The as-long-as-no-one-gets-hurt approach requires an omniscience that none of us possess. It is difficult to see the hurt in the human heart, the damage done to the soul, the sense of regret that often does not manifest itself until later in life. What seems like a good

---

6. About the same time, a massive study on the sex lives of teenagers confirmed that 14 percent of all teenage girls believed it was okay for a girl going steady to have intercourse, but that number shot up to 35 percent "if the girl is in love." (Coles and Stokes, *Sex and the American Teenager*, 47).

idea at the time can often do damage we won't see for decades. We see examples around us every day: using asbestos in house construction, adding lead to increase the durability of paint, creating a permanent dependence on welfare, importing kudzu to stop soil erosion, cross-breeding European honeybees with African honey bees, lying nearly naked in the sun for hours to get a deep tan. These are all things Americans felt very good about at the time, and it didn't seem like anyone would get hurt. Indeed, many of them seemed downright loving. Yet only God is omniscient. He gives his laws knowing all of the consequences, immediate and long-term, of breaking them. In love, he tells us "no."

In the end, it doesn't matter how good you are relative to other people. Nor does it matter how your actions conform to the relative and floating standard of what you sincerely feel is loving and right. By these relative standards, we all can make ourselves look good. What really matters, though, is this: How do you measure up when you are compared to the perfect standard of Jesus Christ?

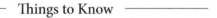

Things to Know

– What are the three abuses of the law?

—— 15 ——

From Despair to Delight

My favorite Bible verse—because I am Christian—is Acts 17:28. It says, 'In God I live and move and have my being' . . . And you want to know why I'm so successful? Because I knew that at 4 years-old . . . I wouldn't be who I am today without a spiritual consciousness, without spiritual values and ultimately without spiritual love.

–OPRAH WINFREY[1]

The law has been given to men for three reasons: 1) to maintain external discipline against unruly and disobedient men, 2) to lead men to a knowledge of their sin, 3) after they are reborn, and although the flesh still inheres in them, to give them on that account a definite rule according to which they should pattern and regulate their entire life.

–FORMULA OF CONCORD, 1577[2]

GOD GAVE THE TEN Commandments to us in a two-table structure. The first four commandments have to do with our relationship with God and the remaining six commandments govern our relationship with each other. Jesus captured this division when he was asked one day, "Which is the greatest commandment?" To answer, Jesus went back into the Old Testament and plucked out Deuteronomy 6:5 and Leviticus 19:18. "You shall love the Lord your God," Jesus replied, "with all your heart and with all your soul and with all your mind. This is the great and first commandment. And a second is like it: You shall love your neighbor as yourself. On these two command-

1. Leclaire, "Oprah Winfrey."
2. Article 6.

ments depend all the Law and the Prophets" (Matt 22:37–40). These are the two summaries of the moral law.

Love God

Can you think of anything more important than understanding what Jesus calls the "first" commandment? Here we are told the essence of what God wants from us.

To love someone is to actively, enthusiastically, and sacrificially seek after their best interests as well as their close presence. To love someone is to desire and pursue their very best and do what brings them joy and happiness. When we love, we delight in the delight of the one we love. Amazingly, we can make decisions that bring God delight and joy and glory (Jer 9:23; Isa 62:5).

We are to love God with all that we are. Heart, soul, and mind do not refer to strictly separate compartments of a human being. Instead, this list refers to the whole being. Emotionally and intellectually, in our feeling and thinking, we are to love him. To love God with our hearts, we engage our emotions, cultivating and directing our affection toward him. God does not want from us a dutiful obedience devoid of warm feelings any more than our wives or children do (Isa 1:11–12), but love is more than warm feelings.

To love him with our mind, we engage our intellect and think deeply *about* him as we study and meditate on his word. Then we think deeply *for* him as we talk about him to others in an effort to bring him glory. In this way, our intellect will inform and govern our emotions, which are so easily deceived by lies and fiction (Jer 17:9).

The wisdom of Jesus in identifying this as the greatest commandment is exquisite. It is possible to obey God and not love him, but it is not possible to love God and not obey him. "If you love me," Jesus said, "you will keep my commandments" (John 14:15). And again, "Whoever has my commandments and keeps them, he it is who loves me" (John 14:21). Love and disobedience cannot coexist.

Love Others

While our love for God comes first, our love for other people comes next. Our neighbors are those who come into our lives. Neighbors are not just family or fellow Christians, but anyone who, in the providence of God, crosses our path. They may be similar to us or very different, but Jesus expects us to love them.

How should we love them? In the same way we love ourselves. We look out for our own best interests rather well. We constantly ask, What can I do for me today? I will have to admit that I consistently choose that which I believe will bring me joy and happiness. When I am tired, I rest. When I am hungry, I eat. When I am cold, I seek warmth. When I have a headache, I take an aspirin. When I am lonely, I call my wife. Jesus is neither condemning nor commanding self-love here. He merely assumes that we all love ourselves.

We should not only consider ourselves, but others. Self-love becomes sinful when we neglect the needs of others. What will make this person happy? What will lead them to joy? How can I serve them? What do they really need that I can give? How can I be the conduit of God's grace to them? This is why the second six commandments can be summed up in this one word: love. It is not loving to dishonor your mother, kill your neighbor, or sleep with your friend's wife. It is not loving to steal or lie or covet. Love is the controlling ethic in all of our relationships.

Love is not just negative, that is, not doing unloving things. Love is also positive, actively doing loving things. For example, it is not just refraining from disrespectful words to your mother-in-law. It is also speaking respectfully to and about her. Love is not just refusing to kill your neighbor. It is also doing those things that help him live longer and better. It is not just refusing to gossip about a competitor. It is also saying things that guard and build his reputation. Love is not just resisting the urge to steal from the rich. It is also sacrificing to give to the poor. This is why Jesus carefully worded what we call The Golden Rule: "So whatever you wish that others would do to you, do also to them, for this is the Law and the Prophets" (Matt 7:12). Notice he did not say: "So whatever you wish others to not do to you, don't do to them." That rule would be easier to keep: Just avoid people as much as possible. The standard Jesus raises requires much more: engage your neighbors, discover their needs, and meet those needs. So, even if we summarize the moral law with these two commands to love, we still find that we don't even come close to keeping them.

At this point, I find some comfort in Jesus' phrase, "On these two commandments depend all the Law and the Prophets" (Matt 22:40). The Greek word for "depend" is sometimes translated as "hang" in the Bible. That's the way it is used in Luke 23:39, where it refers to "one of the criminals who were hanged" on the cross next to Jesus.

Just as Jesus hung on the cross, so all the law hangs on these two commands. Just as one beam of the cross is vertical, pointing heavenward, so the command to love God points us to the first four of the Ten Commandments that have to do with our relationship with God. Just as a second beam of the cross is horizontal, pointing across the earth, so the command to love others points us to the six commandments that govern our relationships with all people. This is a helpful reminder to me that the law leaves me no hope outside of the hope I have in the cross of Christ.

The Three Uses of the Law

In the last chapter, we looked at the three abuses of the law. What, then, is the proper use of the moral law of God? How does God intend for this gift to bring good to us and glory to him? Christians have long noted that there are at least three uses of the moral law of God.

The Civil Use of the Law: To Restrain Evil

In common grace, God shows his kindness to all people, whether they love him or not. Jesus said that the Father "makes his sun rise on the evil and on the good, and sends rain on the just and on the unjust" (Matt 5:45). Every day, believers and unbelievers alike enjoy the gracious benefits of a loving God, even though his gifts are not acknowledged. One of the gifts that God has given to all of us is the moral law. Whether we appeal to the Bible or to common sense, most cultures recognize the wisdom of God's moral law because it is "written on their hearts" (Rom 2:15).

The laws of most lands roughly resemble the second table of the Ten Commandments. In most cultures, for example, many forms of murder, theft, and perjury are prohibited and punished, and there are some basic laws that protect the institution of marriage. Without these laws, and the authority of governments to enforce them, anarchy would reign and society could not survive (Rom 13:1–5). The civil use of the law doesn't make people better, but it causes them to fear the punishment that is meted out by human governments to lawbreakers (Gal 3:19). "The law is good," wrote the apostle Paul, "if one uses it lawfully, understanding this, that the law is not laid down for the just but for the lawless and disobedient, for the ungodly and sinners, for the unholy and profane, for those who strike their fathers and mothers, for murderers, the sexually immoral, men who practice homosexuality, enslavers, liars, perjurers, and whatever else is contrary to sound doctrine" (1 Tim 1:8–10). In short, the civil use of the law is a gift to all humanity that deters crime and curbs evil in the world.

The Convicting[3] Use of the Law: To Point to Christ

When we studied the Ten Commandments in chapter 13, it was painfully clear that none of us could meet God's moral standard. Only a fool will think he can save himself from the wrath of God by his own law-keeping. "All have sinned and fall short," writes Paul, "of the glory of God" (Rom 3:23). It is deadly and unchristian to think we can be "justified by the law" (Gal 5:4).

Without the moral law of God, revealed to us and recorded in Scripture, we would judge ourselves to be good people. Without the law, we would re-sort to guessing where the moral boundaries are. For example, I am confident I could beat you at tennis every time if I constructed the court. On the side of the court I defend, I would put the base and side lines where the regula-tions say they should be. You would be required to return the ball into that small box. On the side of the court you defend, I would put no base or side lines at all. I would only be required to estimate where the ball should land. I'll give myself the benefit of the doubt, of course, and even if it lands in the stands a hundred feet behind you, I'll claim the points. When you finally insist that the lines be drawn on your side as well, we will all see how far I was from meeting the standard. The law gives us the boundary lines, a fixed moral standard, that show us how far we are from living up to the standards God requires of us. This is why Paul could say, "if it had not been for the law, I would not have known sin. For I would not have known what it is to covet if the law had not said, 'You shall not covet'" (Rom 7:7).

Like a skillful prosecutor, the law produces a list of endless indict-ments. Specific charges are linked to indisputable evidence until we are pushed into our *mea culpa*. I am guilty as charged. I cannot rest on my own merit before God, for I have none. I am worthy only of death and hell. At every turn, at some level, I have broken every single commandment of God. I therefore throw myself on the mercy of the court.

The purpose of the law here is to drive us to despair. The law is a mir-ror that lets us see ourselves as we really are. The law is the doctor that gives us the bad news. He is direct, clear, and dismal in his diagnosis. We are infected with a deadly disease. He wants us to fear because we have something that we should be afraid of. This is not a time for platitudes, false hope, and cheap comfort. This is the time for cold, hard truth because if you don't believe you are sick you won't seek a cure. If you don't believe you are in danger, you will not flee to safety. And the good news is this: there is a cure in Christ and safety in the cross.

3. Some theologians refer to this as the "pedagogical" use of the law.

The road of legalism leads to a dead end in hell. Since we cannot save ourselves, we need a Savior. If we don't think we need a Savior, we will not seek him. "The law," wrote Paul, "was our guardian until Christ came, in order that we might be justified by faith" (Gal 3:24). An intellectually honest consideration of the law of God will lead to the only reasonable conclusion: justification by works is hopeless. Justification by faith in Christ is our only hope. Though we cannot hide *from* Christ, we can hide *in* Christ.

The Teaching[4] Use of the Law: To Please God

When a person has come to Christ, trusting in his death on the cross to pay the penalty for his sins, his public profession of faith is the first evidence that he has been "born again" (John 3:3), that is, regenerated. God has created new spiritual life in a person who was once spiritually dead (Col 2:13). Once he is saved by grace through faith, apart from works, he is adopted into the family of God (John 1:12). One of the most reliable tests of whether or not you are a child of God is obedience to the commands of your heavenly Father.

When someone is born again, his whole outlook on the law is changed. Instead of the law being something he has to obey, it is something he wants to obey. Genuine Christians do not keep the law so God will love them. Rather, they keep the law because they love God (John 14:21). Because they love him, they want to please him. Real believers eagerly study the Bible, especially the teaching of the apostles recorded in the New Testament, to discover how they "ought to walk and to please God" (1 Thess 4:1).

For people who have been saved by grace, the law is no longer an enemy who condemns us, but a friend who guides us. "Oh, how I love your law," wrote the psalmist, "It is my meditation all the day" (Ps 119:97). If you really are a child of God, you will "try to discern what is pleasing to the Lord" (Eph 5:10). When you pray, you will ask God to help you "walk in a manner worthy of the Lord, fully pleasing to him" (Col 1:10). When we obey the law's demand to honor our fathers and mothers by taking care of widows and elderly parents, "this is pleasing in the sight of God" (1 Tim 5:4). We do these things because we want to. We want to because we have been born again. We are born again only because of the free grace of God.

---

4. Some theologians refer to this as the "normative" or "didactic" use of the law.

Before we come to Christ, we will hate and abuse the law because it brings us only bad news. After Christ, we will love the law because it shows us how we can please the one we love.

The Tape and the Saw

Which is more important: the tape measure or the saw? Suppose a carpenter wants to frame a house with a saw but no tape measure. He guesses lengths and widths, then makes the cut. Even for the most skilled craftsman, the end result will be an engineering disaster. Not only will he waste a lot of lumber, but the structure will be unsound. Now imagine he tries to frame the house with a tape measure but no saw. He measures, marks, and calculates, but he will never build the house. The tape measure is good at setting the standard, but it was not designed to cut. The saw is good for cutting the wood, but it was not designed to measure. Apart from each other, they are both necessary but insufficient.

Likewise, the law and the gospel work together and neither are to be despised. The law is good at measuring our morality, showing us our faults, and pointing the way, but it is powerless to do anything about our guilt. The gospel has power to remove our guilt, but it is meaningless to someone who does not feel the weight of his sin. The good news will never seem very good to us until the bad news feels very bad to us. This lively partnership of law and gospel is not merely for our initial conversion. Every day, Christians must meditate on the law of God, praying, "Search me, O God, and know my heart! Try me and know my thoughts! And see if there be any grievous way in me and lead me in the way everlasting!" (Ps 139:23–24). When God answers that prayer and shows us where our lives do not measure up to his law, we need not shrivel in fear or stumble under a load of guilt. Because of what Christ has done, we can comfort ourselves with the gospel and "with confidence draw near to the throne of grace, that we may receive mercy and find grace to help in time of need" (Heb 4:16). The next chapter unpacks the beauty of the gospel, how in Christ, the lawgiver became the lawkeeper to save lawbreakers like you and me.

──────────── Things to Know ────────────

- What are the 2 summaries of the law?
- What are the 3 uses of the law?

—— 16 ——

Why Jesus Came

Many have heard the gospel framed in terms of rescue. God has to punish sinners, because God is holy, but Jesus has paid the price for our sin, and so we can
have eternal life. However true or untrue that is technically or theologically,
what it can do is subtly teach people that Jesus rescues us from God. Let's be
very clear, then: we do not need to be rescued from God.

−ROB BELL, FORMER MEGA-CHURCH PASTOR[1]

Every sin, both original and actual, being a transgression of the righteous law
of God, and contrary thereunto, doth, in its own nature, bring guilt upon the
sinner, whereby he is bound over to the wrath of God, and curse of the law, and
so made subject to death, with all miseries spiritual, temporal, and eternal.

−WESTMINSTER CONFESSION, 1647[2]

THE YOUNG MAN HAD a future more significant than any of his questioners
imagined. He was in his senior year at Georgetown University, engaged
in the gut-wrenching capstone of his academic endeavors: comprehensive
oral exams. To graduate, he would need to answer any question from his
teachers about any subject he had studied for the last four years of majoring
in history. Much of that tortuous exercise is a blur to him now, but he will
never forget one question in particular: "If you look back over all the history that you have studied here over the last four years, if you had to pick
one event that you thought was the most significant, what would it be?"

Facing the panel, he mentally sorted through a cascade of possible responses. Could it be the Battle of Waterloo? The Battle of Solomon Islands?

1. Bell, *Love Wins*, 182.
2. 6:6.

To this day, he does not remember his answer. He only remembers that it was wrong. The chairman of the panel sadly shook his head. "No, Mr. Scalia. The Incarnation, Mr. Scalia."

Antonin Scalia, who has served as a Supreme Court Justice since 1986, never forgot the lesson. Never "separate your religious life from your intellectual life."[3] There is, however, a greater lesson still.

Why Did Jesus Come?

The incarnation, God becoming a man in Jesus Christ, is the apex of human history for reasons too many to count here. *That* he came into the world is the subject of no serious debate. Even people who don't believe the incarnation (God in the flesh) believe Jesus, the historical figure, existed. The debate centers on *why* Jesus came into the world. Christians never have to speculate on the answer. The Bible is clear "that Christ Jesus came into the world to save sinners" (1 Tim 1:15). To understand the most important event in history, we need to unpack two words: *save* and *sinners*.

To say someone is a "sinner" is to say he or she has sinned. Sin, writes theologian Wayne Grudem, "is any failure to conform to the moral law of God in act, attitude, or nature."[4] As we have seen in our study of the law, we are all guilty, "for all have sinned" (Rom 3:23). There are no exceptions. Outside of Jesus, no one has ever succeeded in keeping the whole law at every point. We are all guilty. That's the bad news.

The good news is that Jesus came to save guilty sinners like us. That raises the question: Save us from what? Actually, there are several ways to answer that question correctly. Jesus saves us from a lot of things, but all of them have to do with sin. It helps to remember that theologians have long noted three tenses of this salvation.

Three Tenses of Salvation

A Christian can say, "Sometime in the past, God saved me." He normally means that God saved him from the *penalty* of his sin. Since the wages of sin is death (Rom 6:23), we need to be rescued from what we deserve. This is sometimes called the conversion experience and it is a one-time act. This

3. Biskupic, *American Original*, 25.
4. Grudem, *Systematic Theology*, 490.

is when we are regenerated, or born again (John 3:3; Eph 2:5). It is at this point in time that we are justified, or "declared righteous" by God. Speaking of this justification, Paul could say that God "saved us, not because of works done by us in righteousness, but according to his own mercy" (Titus 3:5).

A Christian can also say, "In the present, God is saving me." Paul said "the word of the cross is folly to those who are perishing, but to us who are being saved it is the power of God" (1 Cor 1:18). Though we have been justified and accepted by God for Christ's sake, we still struggle with the power of sin in our life until we die. We will not become *sinless* in this life, but we will *sin less* as we learn to follow Christ and grow in him. By the power of the Holy Spirit, God helps us say no to temptation and break the chains of our addictions, and gradually, by degree, makes us more like Jesus. This process of God making us more holy is called sanctification and it will not be complete until we die or Christ returns.

Finally, a Christian can say, "In the future, God will save me." On some certain and future day, known only to God, Christ will return to "judge the living and the dead" (2 Tim 4:1; 1 Pet 4:5). Genuine Christians who "have now been justified by his blood" will, on that day, "be saved by him from the wrath of God" (Rom 5:9). Though Christians disagree on the exact order of events in the last days, they agree that there is a future day when those Christians who have already died will be raised from the dead and Christians who are alive at his coming will be "caught up together with them in the clouds to meet the Lord in the air" (1 Thess 4:17). All believers will at that time receive new, transformed, immortal, glorified, resurrection bodies, much like the body Jesus received at his own resurrection (1 Cor 15:20–23). This tense of our salvation is sometimes called glorification because at that time we will be saved from the presence of sin forever and we will be "glorified with him" (Rom 8:17).[5]

Justification	Sanctification	Glorification
I was saved from the *penalty* of sin	I am being saved from the *power* of sin	I will be saved from the *presence* of sin
A point in time	A process over a lifetime	A point in time

5. I am not the first to note these tenses or put them in a chart. Like so many other things in this book, these are things I have been taught by others in conversations and classrooms.

So to say that Jesus came to save us from our sins would not be a wrong answer, but the reason our sins are so sinful is that they were committed against a sinless God who is bound by perfect justice to punish them. God is the lawgiver and we are the lawbreakers. Our law breaking requires a just response from the lawgiver who is also the law enforcer. Our sin is an egregious offense against our Creator. He is "of purer eyes than to see evil and cannot look at wrong" (Hab 1:13). In our sinful condition, we are not able to feel the revulsion that God feels when he encounters sin in our own lives or in others. This is because "all the ways of a man are pure in his own eyes" (Prov 16:2). We are easy on ourselves when it comes to judgment.

The next time you are at a big game, no matter the sport, notice how referees or umpires never make everyone happy. When the judgment goes against our team on a questionable call, we are enraged and our opponents are delighted. We view it as a grave injustice while they see it as smart officiating. When the call goes our way, that same referee is brilliant. Even when the referee makes an obvious error in our favor, we happily receive it and celebrate with our friends that we "got away with one."

Here's something you will never see: When a clearly blown call goes your way, you will never see your side explode in moral outrage. You will never see your coach make an angry protest in an effort to help out the opposing coach. You will never hear your fans condemn the great injustice that has just been done to their opponent. We have a sharpened sense of justice when the error is to our disadvantage, but our legal senses are dulled when it is not. "The heart," wrote Jeremiah, "is deceitful above all things, and desperately sick; who can understand it?" (Jer 17:9). The human heart has a limitless capacity for self-justification, self-exoneration, and self-deception.

God as the chief law enforcer never blows a call. He always gets it right. No perjury succeeds, no evidence is suppressed, no bribe is received. He is an impartial judge, and "the wrongdoer will be paid back for the wrong he has done" (Col 3:25). This judge is thoroughly unimpressed and un-intimidated by human pride, power, prestige, and position, so all will be treated equally under the law. He is an omniscient judge, "and no creature is hidden from his sight, but all are naked and exposed to the eyes of him to whom we must give account" (Heb 4:13).

So what is the proper and natural response of sinners when they come to the realization that God hates their sin and owes them only justice? Fear! Jesus could not have been clearer when he said, "do not fear those who kill the body but cannot kill the soul. Rather fear him who can destroy both soul and body in hell" (Matt 10:28).

Hell? Did Jesus really believe in hell? If Jesus didn't, no one ever did. No one in the Bible spoke more of hell than Jesus. Hell is a place of eternal and conscious torment for sinners. John the Baptist's ministry of preparing people for the coming of Christ focused on warning sinners to repent and "flee the wrath to come" (Matt 3:7). In the final judgment, warned Jesus, sinners "will go away into eternal punishment, but the righteous into eternal life" (Matt 25:46). Is hell forever? If hell is not eternal, then neither is heaven. The same word for eternal in this verse is used to describe both destinations.

But wait. Didn't we establish that we are all sinners? If so, all people will go to hell because "none is righteous, no, not one" (Rom 3:10). That is bad news. In fact, it is the worst possible news, but that's where the incarnation, the greatest event in history, crashes in and offers hope. The good news is that Jesus came to give us a righteousness that is not our own. Even though all of us deserve to go to hell, not all of us will. The reason is this: Jesus came to save sinners.

Three Facets of Salvation

Now we turn from the three tenses of salvation to three facets of salvation. Hold a diamond in your hand and you will see one facet. Turn the diamond and you will see another facet. Likewise, the dazzling beauty of salvation is multi-faceted and each side has to be viewed from different angles. In the first facet, we see that we are saved *from* something. In another facet, we see that we are saved *by* something. In a third facet, we are saved *for* something.

We Are Saved From the Wrath God

So let's return to our original question: Christ came to save sinners from what? Now we know the better question is this: Save sinners from *whom*? It is God who gives the law, God who enforces the law, God who is sinned against, God who brings sinners to justice, and God who judges. It is him we ultimately fear. Not any man or woman. Not the devil or his demons. Only God has the authority to judge, condemn, and punish. He has the right, the authority, the grounds, and the means to send us all to hell. All sinners are subject to his wrath so "it is a fearful thing to fall into the hands of the living God (Heb 10:31). For the man who rejects Jesus, "the wrath of God remains on him" (John 3:36), but the man who receives Jesus will be saved by Jesus "from the wrath of God" (Rom 5:9).

The Heidelberg Catechism anticipates and answers a natural question here: "Is not God then also merciful? God is indeed merciful, but he is also righteous. It is his righteousness which requires that sin committed against the supreme majesty of God be punished with extreme, that is, with eternal punishment of body and soul."[6]

In Jesus, God saved us *from* himself.

We Are Saved By the Grace of God

Because of God's wrath, everyone should fear God—but not everyone does. Our modern ears resist language that includes the fear of God, but the fear of God everywhere in the Bible is considered a good thing for several reasons. The fear of God is a gift. Those who genuinely fear God have received an invaluable gift from God. Fear of God can be a sign of God's grace working in your life. This is what John Newton had in mind when he wrote those strange words in the most famous hymn ever written, *Amazing Grace*: "T'was grace that taught my heart to fear, and grace my fears relieved." To fear God's wrath is a precious treasure and a sign that God is lovingly pursuing you. By his grace he is teaching your heart to fear him.

Why is fear of God's wrath a great gift? Among other things, fear is a great motivator. When a doctor sits down with a patient to explain a pathology report that confirms a fast-spreading cancer, one of his aims is to strike fear in the patient. Inciting this fear is the most compassionate thing the doctor can do at this point. If the patient is unafraid, unfazed, unconvinced, the patient will simply not seek a cure. Cancer patients seek treatment because they fear the consequences of doing nothing. Likewise, fear keeps us from dark alleys, off of high cliffs, out of rip tides, and away from snarling pit bulls. A dose of justified terror is a good thing and a gift from God.

In other words, the worst thing that could ever happen to you is that you go through your whole life and never be gripped with fear of God's judgment. That would be a sign that you insanely believe you are not guilty, or at least not guilty enough to be punished. Fearlessness before God is the mark of someone who is blind to his or her own moral condition. Fear is the first step to being reconciled to God. That's why the psalmist can

6. Q. 11.

declare, "Surely his salvation is near to those who fear him" (Ps 85:9), "the friendship of the Lord is for those who fear him" (Ps 25:14), and "the Lord takes pleasure in those who fear him" (Ps 147:11).

Yet one of the first things Jesus said when he calls his disciples is "do not be afraid" (Luke 5:10). How can we sinners really be comfortable in the presence of God incarnate? The answer is love. "There is no fear in love, but perfect love casts out fear. For fear has to do with punishment, and whoever fears has not been perfected in love (1 John 4:18). Perhaps the *best-known* Bible verse is John 3:16: "For God so loved the world, that he gave his only Son, that whoever believes in him should not perish but have eternal life." Perhaps one of the *least-known* Bible verses comes next: "For God did not send his Son into the world to condemn the world, but in order that the world might be saved through him" (John 3:17). The grace that teaches our heart to fear is the same grace that gives our heart the faith to trust him, "for by grace you have been saved through faith. And this is not your own doing; it is the gift of God" (Eph 2:8).

What motivated Jesus to come into the world to save sinners? Love! First, he loved his father who sent him to us. Since love obeys, he was "obedient to the point of death, even death on a cross" (Phil 2:8). Second, he loved and lived out his famous maxim that there is no greater love than for someone to "lay down his life for his friends" (John 15:13). In other words, Jesus obeyed the greatest and second greatest commands: love God with all your heart and love your neighbor as yourself. So grace will teach our hearts to fear, but by grace our fears are relieved in the love of Jesus. Jesus, being God in the flesh, is the one who saves us. Therefore, we are saved *from* God *by* God.

Former mega-church pastor Rob Bell doesn't like this very much and seeks to persuade his readers that this truth is inconsistent with the character of God: "And so what gets subtly sort of caught and taught is that Jesus rescues you from God. But what kind of God is that, that we would need to be rescued from this God?"[7] In direct contradiction with the winsome yet misleading words of Rob Bell, Scripture is clear that the God we worship is a God from whom we needed to be rescued. Jesus came to rescue us from God.

In Jesus, God saved us *by* himself.

---

7. Barrick, "Rob Bell Gets Evangelicals."

We Are Saved For the Glory of God

We are not just saved *from* God but also *for* God. We are not just saved *from* experiencing the wrath of God. We are saved *for* experiencing the love of God. We are not just saved *from* death, but we are also saved *for* life. God purchases us so that we might be his people, "a chosen race, a royal priesthood, a holy nation, a people for his own possession" (1 Pet 2:9). God rescues us so he can adopt us and make us "the children of God" (John 1:12). He gives us a heart to love him, a mind to know him, the ability to serve him, a desire to obey him, and a capacity to enjoy him. This is what we were made to do and until we do it, we will never know real peace and contentment. "Thou has made us for thyself," cried out Augustine in prayer, "and restless is our heart until it comes to rest in thee."[8] "What is the chief end of man?" asks the Westminster Shorter Catechism. "Man's chief end is to glorify God, and to enjoy him forever." God made us for his glory (Isa 43:7) and in the words of John Piper, "God is most glorified in me when I am most satisfied in him."[9]

In Jesus, God saved us *for* himself.

Antonin Scalia was right to say that the incarnation is the most significant event in human history, but the incarnation is not necessarily the gospel. That God came to us in flesh does not, in itself, help our plight. It's what he did once he got here. In Jesus, God freely saved us *from* himself, *by* himself, *for* himself. That's really good news.

───────── Things to Know ─────────

- What are the 3 tenses of salvation?
- What are the 3 facets of salvation?

8. Augustine, *Confessions and Enchiridion*, Book 1, Chapter 1.
9. Piper, *Desiring God*, 9.

—— 17 ——

What is the Gospel?

I wouldn't consider myself a theologian, and I don't debate Scripture. I feel like what I'm good about, and I think this is the one reason the ministry is successful, I talk about how do we live the Christian life, how do we forgive, how do we have a good self-image.

—JOEL OSTEEN, PASTOR OF THE LARGEST CHURCH IN AMERICA[1]

Question 71: May we not gather from this what fruit we receive from the death of Christ? Yes, indeed. And, first, we see that it is a sacrifice by which he has made satisfaction for us before the judgment of God, and so has appeased the wrath of God and reconciled us to him.

—GENEVA CATECHISM, 1536

THE GOSPEL IS NOT about something we have done for God, but something God has done for us. In fact, the gospel is not about our doing anything. It's not about our living the Christian life. It's not about our forgiving other people. It's not about working on our self-image. It is all about the life that Christ lived, the forgiveness he offers, and the work he accomplished. The gospel is not about you; it is about him. While it is true that you must respond to the gospel with repentance and faith, your response is not the gospel. It may also be true that you have a personal story, a testimony, unique to you, of how you have experienced God's grace, but your testimony is not the gospel. The gospel is not your story, but God's story. The gospel must be the central message of every man who claims to follow Christ, for there is no news that is good news apart from the good news of the gospel.

1. Killough, "Osteen: Romney is a Christian."

That God has saved sinners from himself, by himself, and for himself is good news, but it is not all the good news. The gospel (which literally means "good news") also includes *how* God has saved us. What is it that Christ did to save us? Specifically, he did four things that are clearly presented in 1 Corinthians 15:1–6:

> Now I would remind you, brothers, of the gospel I preached to you, which you received, in which you stand, and by which you are being saved, if you hold fast to the word I preached to you—unless you believed in vain. For I delivered to you as of first importance what I also received:
>> that Christ died for our sins in accordance with the Scriptures,
>> that he was buried,
>> that he was raised on the third day in accordance with the Scriptures, and
>> that he appeared to Cephas, then to the twelve. Then he appeared to more than five hundred brothers at one time, most of whom are still alive, though some have fallen asleep.

Notice that the gospel is not a command, but a statement. It is not a directive, but an announcement. It is not an imperative, but an indicative. It is a historical event, not a self-help technique. The gospel is the happy declaration that Jesus Christ did four things in order to save sinners.

The first element of the gospel is that Jesus died for our sins. On the cross, Jesus became our substitute, the sacrificial Lamb of God who "takes away the sins of the world" (John 1:29). Paul can say that this was "in accordance with the Scriptures" because the Old Testament had predicted and foreshadowed this vicarious atonement at every turn (e.g., Isa 53). As we saw in chapters 12–15, the ceremonial law, the sacrificial system of the Old Testament, prepared God's people for the final sacrifice and ultimate high priest. On the cross, the wrath of God was satisfied, the justice of God was executed, the favor of God was regained, and the love of God was most dramatically revealed (Heb 2:17; 1 John 4:10). The blood of Jesus purchased the church (Acts 20:28), cancelled out our debt to God (Col 2:14), and provided the just grounds on which God forgives repentant sinners (Rom 3:25–26).

In heaven, a recurring song of praise most certainly will be "Worthy is the Lamb who was slain, to receive power and wealth and wisdom and might and honor and glory and blessing!" (Rev 5:12). "Worthy are you to take the scroll and to open its seals, for you were slain, and by your blood you ransomed people for God from every tribe and language and people and nation" (5:9). On the cross, Jesus absorbed the wrath of God for sin and satisfied God's demands for justice (Rom 3:25). Though he was without sin, he took our sin on himself, and received what guilty sinners deserve.

The second element of the gospel is that Jesus was buried. It may seem strange that the burial of Christ is counted by Paul as part of the gospel. How is a burial good news? The burial of Christ is recounted in significant detail in the Bible. His body had suffered severe trauma in a pre-crucifixion scourging and then the wrists and ankles were pierced with nails. After several hours on the cross, Jesus likely died of asphyxiation as it became impossible to breathe. The gospels assert that after Jesus took his last breath on the cross, a soldier confirmed his death by piercing the side of Jesus with a spear. From that incision poured out the fluid of the pericardial sac (John 19:34).

On Friday afternoon, the body was removed from the cross and tightly wrapped in linen cloth and spices (John 19:40). This Jewish custom would have bound up Jesus' limbs, covered his face, and added up to 100 pounds to his body weight. His bound body was then placed in a tomb, which was carved into rock, and a stone, weighing as much as a half-ton, was rolled across the opening (Matt 27:60). Yet, the Jewish religious leaders were concerned that the disciples would steal the body in the night, and then claim Jesus had risen from the dead. To prevent this scenario, the governor Pilate authorized a Roman military guard to protect the tomb. The body of Jesus was in the tomb from Friday evening until Sunday morning. That same Roman guard witnessed an angel rolling back the stone and announcing to Mary Magdalene and the other Mary that Jesus had been raised from the dead (Matt 28:1–15).

Why do the gospel writers give all these details about the burial of Christ? The apostles, who were eyewitnesses to the risen Lord, want their readers to know that Jesus had not merely fainted. He had not temporarily lost consciousness. He was not revived in the coolness of the tomb (albeit drained of his blood), only to rip through the linen cloth, roll back a mammoth stone, beat off a band of well-armed professional soldiers, and start a new religion, based on a lie, that would lead to the martyrdom of his closest friends. No, Jesus was dead. He was stone cold dead. And his burial proves it.

The third element is that Jesus was raised from the dead. If the incarnation is the greatest event in all of history, the resurrection of Christ is arguably the greatest event of the incarnation. It is a pivotal point in the history of the world, and nothing has been the same since. Watching the death of Christ did not empower his disciples. Rather, it deflated them. When Jesus died, so did their dreams and hopes for the future. The dying of

Jesus, as significant as it is, did not inspire his disciples to take the teachings of Jesus to the world. While Jesus died, they denied him, abandoned him, and cowered in fear. What changed their lives? What turned this marginalized band of fisherman and tax collectors into a motivated team that would change the course of history? The answer is the resurrection of Christ. The resurrection is the kingpin of the Christian faith. "If Christ has not been raised," conceded Paul, "then our preaching is in vain" (1 Cor 15:14).

Among other things, the resurrection is a proof of purchase. Jesus claimed to be the Messiah, not only a spokesman for God, but God himself. Others had claimed to be the Messiah before he died and more have since, but it's one thing to make an audacious claim and another to prove it. How do we know Jesus was telling the truth? How do we know that God accepted the death of Jesus as payment for our sins? Once again, the answer is the resurrection.

By raising him from the dead, God is accommodating our need for evidence. By raising him from the dead, God is giving us abundant reasons to believe that his death satisfied God's demand for justice. Those who put their faith in Christ's finished work on the cross can also look forward to their own resurrection in the future. They are convinced of their own resurrection because "Christ has been raised from the dead" (1 Cor 15:20). Likewise, the return of Christ to judge the living and the dead is something we can depend on because God "has given assurance to all by raising him from the dead" (Acts 17:31).

If you live long enough, you will buy something you will want to return. It may be clothes that don't fit you or a gadget that won't work, but when you take it back to the store, you will need proof that you paid for it. So when you return your item, you will also produce a receipt. That receipt is the hard physical evidence that the item indeed belongs to you. That same receipt will let you walk out the door, unchallenged by store security, with your purchase in hand. When God purchased his people with the blood of his Son, he got what he wanted. As broken as we are, he will never return us for we are eternally secure in his love. Nonetheless, God proves to the world that he loves us that much by producing the ultimate receipt. The proof of purchase was not paper and ink, but flesh and blood, the resurrected body of Jesus Christ.

The fourth element of the gospel is the post-resurrection appearances to many eyewitnesses. After all, what good would the resurrection do if no one saw it? Paul refers to over five hundred eyewitnesses to the resurrection.

Importantly, he notes that most of them are still alive when he was writing. That is significant because there are many people who could confirm or deny Paul's testimony. While many historians have doubted whether Jesus was raised from the dead, no serious historian doubts that the earliest followers of Jesus firmly *believed* he was raised from the dead. They believed this, the earliest followers said, because they saw him.

Why should we believe their testimony? Anyone can claim to see anything, after all. Fair enough, but few maintain their testimony in the face of suffering. If they were lying, what was their motive? Publicly claiming to see the risen Lord did not make the disciples healthy or wealthy. It made them sick and poor. Those original disciples lost their health, their wealth, their social status, their freedom, and eventually, most of them lost their lives, all because they claimed to be eyewitnesses of his resurrection.

Someone might say, people die for sincerely held religious beliefs all the time. When a man straps explosives on his body and blows himself up in a marketplace, he might do so because he is very committed to his religion. That's true, of course, but that is not what the disciples did. While many people die for what they believe is true, no one dies for what they know is false. If Jesus was not raised from the dead, and the disciples fabricated a story saying he did, then no one knew better than they that Christianity was predicated on a lie. And yet, they maintained their testimony to their dying breath.

So the gospel has four elements:

1. Christ died to pay the penalty of our sins.

2. Christ was buried to prove he had died.

3. Christ was raised to prove his payment for sins was accepted.

4. Christ appeared to many eyewitnesses to prove he was raised.

Your response is not the gospel. One of the most common mistakes that Christian men will make in bearing witness to Christ is to present their response to the gospel instead of the gospel. I once heard a well-respected NFL player give his testimony in which he recounted a vague emotional experience in church one day as a teenager in which he "accepted Jesus into his heart." He talked about how he started living his life differently, how he tries not to cuss in front of teammates, how he loves his wife and kids. These are all admirable things and I have high regard for his integrity, on and off of the field. He still has a good reputation in the league. Not once, however, did he mention the substitutionary death and the validating resurrection of

Jesus Christ. He talked much of himself and his response to the gospel (his feelings, his change of life, his sense of purpose), but he never proclaimed the gospel. Always remember that if you give a talk, a testimony, or a teaching and you never mention the cross and what was accomplished there, whatever you just shared with those people was not the gospel.

That a holy God has drawn near to us is not in itself good news. In fact, it is the worst possible news for guilty sinners. Why would a criminal welcome the police? No, the coming of Christ is very bad news, unless the sinner repents. If he or she turns from trusting in false gods, manmade idols, good works, religious rituals, and self-righteousness and turns to trust in Christ alone, then the incarnation is good news. Follow the evidence and the conclusion is this: We cannot save ourselves. We will never be smart enough, good enough, or strong enough to rescue ourselves from this dire predicament. The Supreme Judge of the universe declares us guilty. Since we cannot save ourselves, we desperately need a Savior.

True Christians know the only thing they deserve from God is punishment. There is no one in hell who does not deserve to be there, and there is no one in heaven who does. These are sobering and painful truths, but embracing these truths is a necessary step toward being reconciled to God. The good news will never be good to you if the bad news is never real to you. Only when the bad news is real to you will you turn to the only way of escape God has provided: Christ alone.

Things to Know

–   What are the 4 elements of the gospel?

—— 18 ——

Ad Fontes!

What I believe in is that if I live my life as well as I can, that I will be rewarded. I don't presume to have a knowledge of what happens after I die . . . [Sin is] being out of alignment with my values.

—BARAK OBAMA, PRESIDENT OF THE UNITED STATES[1]

We are accounted righteous before God, only for the merit of our Lord and Savior Jesus Christ by faith, and not for our own works or deservings: Wherefore that we are justified by faith only is a most wholesome doctrine, and very full of comfort.

—*CHURCH OF ENGLAND,* THIRTY-NINE ARTICLES, 1571

I WAS BORN IN St. Louis, not far from the banks of the Mississippi River. I remember as a boy looking down on its foamy current from the top of the Gateway Arch during the spring floods. The water resembled chocolate milk, choked with all manner of debris. In flood season, the river sweeps away whole trees, chunks of plastic, and unidentified floating objects. What I could not see then were the countless gallons of chemicals dumped by factories, fertilizer runoff from farms, and flotsam expelled from a hundred sewage treatment plants upstream along the Mississippi and Missouri River Valleys. Altogether, the Mississippi drains 40 percent of the continental United States. The thought never occurred to me that I should go down to its banks to satisfy my thirst.

It's a different story upstream. Twenty-five hundred miles north of the Gulf of Mexico, you can step across the Mississippi River at its source in Minnesota. By one account, the source of the Mississippi is Lake Itasca,

---

1. Foust, "Obama: Sin Is."

which derives its name from combining the last four letters of the Latin word for truth (*veritas*) with the first two letters of the Latin word for head or source (*caput*). Taken together, Itasca means "the source of truth." By other accounts, the source of the Mississippi River begins with any number of crystal clear streams that flow into Lake Itasca. No matter which theory you subscribe to, the point is the same. Would you rather drink from the Mississippi in New Orleans or Minnesota? Information is like a river. The closer you can get to the source, the better.

Five Slogans of the Reformation

Even if you do not consider yourself a protestant, an evangelical, or even an heir of the protestant tradition, you still need to know what the Reformation was about. It is one of the most important events in history, and knowing its features is part of being an educated person.

Though there had been many attempts at reform within the church through the centuries, October 31, 1517, is the date that most historians view as a critical turning point. On that day, Martin Luther, an Augustinian monk in the Roman Catholic Church, posted ninety-five theses on the door of the Castle Church in Wittenberg, Germany.[2] Nothing has been the same since.

The Reformers did not *discover* any great truths. Rather they *recovered* great truths that had been crusted over by centuries of human tradition. They did not create something new. Rather they restated something old. This was the period of the Renaissance and the rallying cry among scholars in Europe was *ad fontes!,* which means "to the sources." It was a period of fresh appreciation for the Greek and Latin classics.

For theologians like Martin Luther, it meant getting underneath Latin translations of the Scriptures and studying the New Testament in the original Greek and the Old Testament in the original Hebrew. Instead of relying on interpretations of church fathers, creeds, and councils, the reformers used them as guides, but went back to the Scripture itself and the languages in which it was originally written. The guiding principle was that solid knowledge is based on the earliest and best sources. They wanted to drink from the Mississippi in Minnesota. For Luther and the reformers, this study

---

2. Posting on a church door was the standard method scholars used to announce topics they wanted to formally debate. Most of the topics in Luther's theses dealt with the corruption of the church and the abuse perpetrated by Pope Leo X.

of Scripture, especially the letters of Romans and Galatians, began a journey that led, among other things, to the recovery of five central truths of the Christian faith.

Why does Paul tell the Corinthians they are to "hold to the word I preached to you" (1 Cor 15:2)? It is because they were in danger of accepting "a different gospel" (2 Cor 11:4). Likewise, Paul was shocked at how quickly the Galatians had received "a different gospel" (Gal 1:6). There is a natural tendency to drift from these doctrines on salvation. Our default religion is legalism, seeking to merit the love and favor of God through law-keeping. Legalism fosters human pride and creates an atmosphere of manipulation.

When religious leaders convince people that they can manipulate God by keeping his rules, it becomes easier for religious leaders to manipulate people. To gain power and control over people, it is important to keep them biblically illiterate and ignorant of the teachings of grace. By abusing the law, they can persuade people that their own words and interpretation of Scripture are equal in authority to Scripture itself. By creating an elaborate hierarchical system, leaders are positioned to reap a financial and political profit. Eventually, hypocritical religious activity eclipses the glorious gospel, and the church is fraught with corruption. For this reason, Christian voices from the past remind us that the church must be *semper reformanda*, "always reforming."

No church, Catholic or Protestant, is immune to the seduction. We must always "be alert" (Acts 20:31), "keep awake" (1 Thess 5:6), "be diligent" (2 Pet 3:14), "test everything" (1 Thess 5:21), especially when it comes to the gospel (1 Cor 15:2). And when a different gospel infiltrates the church (as it certainly will), it must be removed before it corrupts the whole assembly. Throughout church history, five pillars of truth, captured in five slogans, have been repeatedly recovered in order to guard the gospel. These are the five slogans of the Reformation:

According to the authority of *Scripture alone,*
we are saved by *grace alone,*
through *faith alone,*
in *Christ alone,*
to *the glory of God alone.*

Scripture Alone (sola scriptura)

When the Apostle Paul brought the gospel to Berea (in modern Greece), Luke praises the Jews there because "they received the word with all eagerness, examining the Scriptures daily to see if these things were so" (Acts 17:11). There is no higher authority than Scripture. God's Word stands alone as the final authority in all matters of belief and behavior. No man or woman, no matter how eloquent or persuasive, has greater authority than Scripture. All statements made about God or on behalf of God are evaluated by the standard of Scripture. No creed or council, no pope or preacher is equal to or above the Word of God. All churches and every church leader must submit to the authority of Scripture. In the words of New Hampshire Baptists in 1833, the Scripture is "the true center of Christian union, and the supreme standard by which all human conduct, creeds, and opinions should be tried."[3]

Grace Alone (sola gratia)

Grace translates a Greek word that means "gift." A gift is free, undeserved, and unearned. That doesn't mean it's cheap. The salvation God gives to us is priceless and it cost him dearly. "For the wages of sin is death," Paul contends, "but the free gift of God is eternal life in Christ Jesus our Lord" (Rom 6:23). That's why he insists that it is "by grace you have been saved through faith. And this is not your own doing; it is the gift of God, not a result of works, so that no one may boast" (Eph 2:8). Even the faith you put in Christ is a gift from God. You would have no faith to put in him if he had not given it to you. Eternal life is a free gift. Reconciliation with God is a free gift. Forgiveness is a free gift. God owes us nothing except judgment, death, and hell. Yet God graciously gives justification, life, and heaven to everyone who believes in his Son. The way God saves us leaves no room for human boasting (1 Cor 1:29).

Faith Alone (sola fide)

While the doctrine of scripture alone was the formal cause of the Reformation, the material cause was the doctrine of justification by faith alone.

---

3. New Hampshire Confession, 1833, Article 1.

What does justification mean? The Westminster Shorter Catechism offers this Scripture-soaked answer:

"Justification is an act of God's free grace, wherein he pardons all our sins, and accepts us as righteous in His sight, only for the righteousness of Christ imputed to us, and received by faith alone."[4]

To be justified is to be "declared righteous." We receive this justification, which is the basis of our salvation, by faith. The Greek word *pisteuo*, is translated two ways in English. When it is used as a noun, the word is "faith." When it is used as a verb, the word is "believe." So when you see "faith" and "believe" in the New Testament, you are looking at the same Greek word. For example, when the Philippian jailer asks Paul and Silas, "What must I do to be saved?" they do not hesitate to say, "Believe in the Lord Jesus, and you will be saved" (Acts 16:30–31). That is another way to say, "Put your faith in Jesus."

To understand what it means to be justified by faith alone, it might help to clarify three competing ideas. These three alternatives are rejected by Scripture.

Counterfeit #1: Works → Justification

This is a form of legalism that we have already discussed. Most of the world's religions are based on the idea that if adherents do good work, keep God's laws, follow some form of the Golden Rule, or accumulate good karma, then God or the gods or some higher power or principle will reward them with a declared righteousness. Most religions include some measure of grace because everyone knows they are not perfect. These religions teach that people are able to do enough good things to cancel out the bad things they've done. In this view, good works are put on one side of the scale and evil deeds are put on the other side. At the end of life, God (or whatever) weighs your works. If you have more good works than evil deeds, you get to go to heaven, nirvana, paradise, or some other eternal vacation. If your evil deeds outweigh your good works, your destiny is not so nice.

Scripture clearly contradicts this way of thinking: "we know that a person is not justified by works of the law but through faith in Jesus Christ, so we also have believed in Christ Jesus, in order to be justified by faith in Christ and not by works of the law, because by works of the law no one will be justified" (Gal 2:16). And again, "For by grace you have been saved

4. Q:33.

through faith. And this is not your own doing; it is the gift of God, not a result of works, so that no one may boast" (Eph 2:8–9).

Counterfeit #2: Faith + Works → Justification

When people who have practiced legalism encounter the gospel, real grace is a hard thing to grasp. There are features of the gospel that are appealing, but our human pride makes us reluctant to admit we are completely incompetent when it comes to obeying the law. We know we are not perfect, and we need a little help, so we blend our natural legalism with the gospel to create a partnership with God. Essentially, we are saying, "I do my best, God does the rest." Maybe you sincerely try hard and obey the law 80% of the time (I'm being generous). Now God kicks in 20% and you're all good. You can be thankful to God for his part in your salvation, but you can get some credit too. Or maybe you do your best, and you score 20%. In that case, God makes up the 80% difference. That makes you a lot more grateful, but you still make a sizable contribution to your salvation. In this scheme, you're saved by *some* grace, but not by grace *alone*.

It's like that awkward moment in a restaurant when the waiter brings the check. Your friend grabs it and insists on buying your lunch, but you are not entirely comfortable with that arrangement so you say, "I'll get the tip." That eases your mind a bit, since you contribute something. In the end, you are not trusting your friend to pay for it all.

If you and I go skydiving and I hand you a parachute and tell you I packed it myself, you may want a few more details. You would want to know about my training and experience. You would also want to know where the reserve chute is located. If you attach a reserve chute to your harness, you are not trusting in me and my work. You are adding to it. That may be wise when we are talking about trusting people (especially in skydiving situations), but foolish when we are talking about trusting God.

If we believe we are justified by our faith in Christ *plus* our good works, we are saying that Christ's good works are deficient. They are not good enough. His death on the cross fell short. In this scheme, Christ's work on the cross must be supplemented by my work. Yet Paul is clear that good works do not belong on this side of the equation. Our salvation is in no sense "a result of works" and if it were, we would have grounds to boast (Eph 2:9). We would boast about our 80% or our 20% but we would certainly boast. Yet there will be no boasting in heaven (1 Cor 1:29). Paul is the model for every Christian when he declared "far be it from me to boast except in the cross of our Lord Jesus Christ" (Gal 6:14).

Counterfeit #3: Faith → Justification

This formula is a corruption of *sola fide*. It recognizes that we are justified by faith alone, but it seeks to abuse the grace of God. The grace abuser hears the gospel and thinks, "This will be a great arrangement. I'm good at sinning and God is good at forgiving." He thinks that if he just believes Christ died to pay his sins, he now has a license to sin. He reasons that if good works are not a condition for our justification, then good works are not necessary in our justification.

Paul meets this challenge head on when he asks, "What shall we say then? Are we to continue in sin that grace may abound? By no means! How can we who died to sin still live in it?" (Rom 6:1–2). If we are in Christ, then we are new creations (2 Cor 5:17). God will change us and give us new hearts. No longer are the commands of God something we *have* to do. Now they are something we *want* to do. When we see what Christ has done for us, we will love him, and if we love him, we will want to please him. If we want to please him, we will obey him by doing good works (John 14:21). If we do not want to please him, this is evidence that we do not know him.

This is the heresy James is addressing when he offers this challenge: "So also faith by itself, if it does not have works, is dead. Show me your faith apart from your works, and I will show you my faith by my works" (Jas 2:17–18).

Authentic Christianity: Faith → Justification + Works

The Reformers worked tirelessly to recover and revere the truth that faith alone results in justification plus good works. Here good works are necessary, but instead of being the necessary *condition* of our justification, they are the necessary *consequence*. We are not saved because we do good works; we do good works because we are saved. Good works are the evidence to the world that we have been justified in God's sight. This is why Jesus constantly reminded his disciples to look beyond what people say about their relationship with God. You can recognize a true or false teacher "by their fruits" (Matt 7:20). Not just what they say, but what they do. The world would know that they were his disciples not just by what they said, but by their love for one another expressed in tangible ways (John 13:35). It's often been said that we are justified by faith alone, but not by faith that is alone. Genuine saving faith is always accompanied by good works that validate a man's claim to belong to God.

While grace abusers may be fond of the truth in Ephesians 2:8–9, they tend to ignore the next verse: "For we are his workmanship, created in Christ Jesus for good works, which God prepared beforehand, that we should walk in them" (Eph 2:10). The Thirty-nine Articles of the Church of England demonstrate the proper balance when they assert that "we are justified by faith only"[5] but also that "good works, which are the fruits of faith, and follow after justification, cannot put away our sins, and endure the severity of God's judgment; yet are they pleasing and acceptable to God in Christ, and do spring out necessarily of a true and lively faith insomuch that by them a lively faith may be as evidently known as a tree discerned by the fruit."[6]

Counterfeit #1	Works → Justification
Counterfeit #2	Faith + Works → Justification
Counterfeit #3	Faith → Justification
Authentic Christianity	Faith → Justification + Works[7]

Christ Alone (solus Christus)

What about all the sincere people in the world who hold to different religions? Does Christ offer the only way to be reconciled to God? To say yes is to open ourselves to the charge of arrogant intolerance. To say no is to deny the Scriptures and betray Christ. Jesus was clear when he said, "I am the way, and the truth, and the life. No one comes to the Father except through me" (John 14:6). Peter was plain when he said, "there is salvation in no one else, for there is no other name under heaven given among men by which we must be saved" (Acts 4:12). Paul could reason that if there was some other way to be reconciled to God, "then Christ died for no purpose" (Gal 2:21). To say there is another way is to question the character of God who sent his precious Son to die in blood and agony for nothing. If there was some other way, the Father would have said, "Take that way, and spare my

---

5. Article 11.

6. Article 12.

7. Gerstner, *A Primer on Justification*, 2–24.

Son!" Yet, he "did not spare his own Son but gave him up for us all" (Rom 8:32). Why? Because we can only be reconciled to God by Christ alone.

Is it really arrogant to make this claim? Some Christians may speak this truth in an arrogant way, but if they do, they shouldn't. Jesus and the apostles repeatedly warn Christians to be humble both before God and man. We are asked to defend our faith clearly and competently, yet "with gentleness and respect" (1 Pet 3:15). Likewise, church leaders should correct their theological opponents "with gentleness" (2 Tim 2:25). Humility is the hallmark of walking with Christ and a prominent Christian virtue (Eph 4:2; Phil 2:3; Col 3:12; Jas 4:6).

That being said, it would be the height of arrogance to contradict Jesus and tell people merely what they want to hear. It would also be unloving to Christ and people. Though some Christians have arrogant methods, our message is not arrogant if it is true. When Paul arrived in the city of Athens and observed the sincerely held religious beliefs among its citizens, he did not conclude that they had merely arrived at some alternative way of being reconciled to God. He did not think to himself, "Well, as long as these people are sincere and try their best to be good and are deeply religious, they should be okay." Instead, "his spirit was provoked within him as he saw that the city was full of idols" (Acts 17:16). And then he preached the gospel to them and urged them to turn to Christ alone.

The framers of the Westminster Larger Catechism are consistent with Scripture when they write that those who have never heard the gospel, or those who do not believe in Jesus Christ "cannot be saved . . . neither is there salvation in any other, but in Christ alone, who is the Savior only of his body the church."[8] Likewise, the Thirty-Nine Articles state that Christians must not say that people who sincerely practice other religions will be saved, no matter how sincere or devout, "for Holy Scripture doth set out unto us only the Name of Jesus Christ, whereby men must be saved."[9] Therefore, Jesus is not a *good* way to get to heaven. Jesus is not the *best* way to get to heaven. Jesus is the *only* way to get to heaven.

Glory of God Alone (soli Deo gloria)

Our salvation is not a joint effort between God and us. God starts it, sustains it, and completes it. It's not a matter of us doing our best and God

8. Question 60.
9. Article 18.

doing the rest. God does it all. Yes, we are responsible to respond to the gospel, to receive it, but even then, we are enabled to respond by God. We don't make ourselves spiritually alive. Rather God makes us alive so we can respond to the gospel (Eph 2:5). We don't cause ourselves to be born again, any more than we caused ourselves to be born. Rather God causes us to be born again, regenerates us, so we can see the gospel for the truth it is (John 3:3). If God does all the work, then it is only right that God gets all the glory. The salvation offered to us in Scripture exalts God and humbles us. It shows that he is big and we are small. He is strong and we are weak. He is wise and we are foolish. He is all and we are nothing.

After laying out a meticulous treatise on our salvation in Christ, Paul can no longer contain his joy as he explodes in praise,

> For who has known the mind of the Lord, or who has been his counselor? Or who has given a gift to him that he might be repaid? For from him and through him and to him are all things. To him be glory forever. Amen. (Rom 11:34–36)

In 1731, forty-five years before the Declaration of Independence was signed, Jonathan Edwards, America's greatest theologian, said it like this:

> So much the more men exalt themselves, so much the less will they surely be disposed to exalt God. It is certainly what God aims at in the disposition of things in redemption . . . that God should appear full, and man in himself empty, that God should appear all, and man nothing. It is God's declared design that others should not "glory in his presence," which implies that it is his design to advance his own comparative glory. So much the more man "glories in God's presence," so much the less glory is ascribed to God.[10]

William Temple, the Archbishop of the Church of England during World War II, said it like this: "all is of God; the only thing of my very own which I contribute to my redemption is the sin from which I need to be redeemed."[11] What could be more God-exalting and man-humbling than this? The only thing we contribute to our salvation is the sin which made it necessary? Since God did all the work in our salvation, it is only right that he should get all the glory.

If you put in a canoe at St. Louis you have to make a decision. Upstream or downstream? The easiest thing is to point the canoe toward New

10. Edwards, *Works*, 2:6.
11. Cited in Stott, *Cross of Christ*, 197.

Orleans and go with the flow. It will take little effort on your part if you have the time. There are no Class Five rapids. No portages. No resistance. Just drift, farther and farther from the source, as the way to the Gulf gets wider.

Getting to the headwaters, on the other hand, takes work. It requires effort that few are willing to give. Upstream, against the current, the way only becomes more narrow. If you want to experience the Mississippi in its purest form, you have to head to Itasca, the "source of truth." Information is like a river. The closer you can get to the source, the better. *Ad fontes!*

———————— Things to Know ————————

– What are the 5 slogans of the Reformation?

19

The Great Exchange

I don't believe in a heaven or a hell or an old man sitting on a throne. I believe in a higher power bigger than me because that keeps me accountable. Accountability is rare to find, especially with people like myself, because nobody wants to tell you something you don't want to hear.

−KATY PERRY, RECORDING ARTIST, ACTRESS[1]

Question 1: What is your only comfort in life and in death? That I belong—body and soul, in life and in death—not to myself but to my faithful Savior, Jesus Christ, who at the cost of his own blood has fully paid for my sins and has completely freed me from the dominion of the devil; that he protects me so well that without the will of my Father in heaven not a hair can fall from my head; indeed that everything must fit his purpose for my salvation. Therefore, by his Holy Spirit, he also assures me of eternal life, and makes me wholeheartedly willing and ready from now on to live for him.

−THE HEIDELBERG CATECHISM, 1563

THE BIBLE PAINTS A bleak picture of our spiritual condition before we came to Christ. We were enemies (Rom 5:10), sons of the devil (John 8:44), children of wrath (Eph 2:3), and spiritually dead (Col 2:13). No one had to teach us how to sin. It just came naturally. Every parent knows that every baby is born self-centered and self-absorbed. You will rarely scold your child for sharing too many of his things or caring too much for others. Small children rarely thank their mothers for all they do for them, and then tell Mom to go to bed early while they wash the dishes for her. These are things

---

1. Hoffman, "Katy Conquers All."

that must be taught and reinforced constantly. Not so with sinning. You will never have to teach your children to be more selfish or to hoard their toys. They will naturally look out for themselves without regard for others. There will be moments of apparent altruism as they reflect the residual image of God, but those moments will be remarkable and unusual.

Children will intentionally sin against God as soon as they are able. They will do something they know they should not do. They will prove that they are conscious of their guilt by trying to hide their deed. They will cover up and lie and deceive because they know in their hearts they have done something wrong. There are no exceptions to this, as much as you would like to think your child is exceptional. Everyone sins very early. Why?

The First Imputation: Adam's Guilt to Us

The Psalmist declares "Behold, I was brought forth in iniquity, and in sin did my mother conceive me" (Ps 51:5). In the beginning something went terribly wrong. "In Adam all die," wrote Paul (1 Cor 15:22). Adam was our perfect representative and did exactly what we would have done. As a consequence of his sin, all of his descendants are fallen and no part of our being is unaffected.

It is not that we are as bad as we can possibly be. We are all made in the image of God and the vestiges of that image remain. Unbelievers all over the world who do not know Christ still display traces of the honor and dignity and beauty of God's image. There are many honorable non-Christians who love their families and deal fairly in the market place and show mercy to orphans. Yet because we are fallen, all of our good works are tainted. Even when we do the right thing, our motives are mixed. We fall so short of God's standard that it is not biblically correct to say that anyone is good. In fact, Jesus said that "no one is good except God alone" (Luke 18:19).

So we are born guilty because in Adam "all sinned" (Rom 5:12). Adam's trespass "led to the condemnation for all men" (Rom 5:18), and by Adam's disobedience "many were made sinners" (Rom 5:18). We are born with corrupted bodies and souls that will fail us. We are all quite dysfunctional, and often feel a battle of conflicting desires within us. We are broken from the beginning. Why are we like this? It is because Adam's sin was imputed to all of his descendants and every generation has proven their fallenness by personally, actually sinning as soon as they are aware of right and wrong. We are born this way because of the imputation of Adam's guilt to us.

To "impute" means to credit, attribute, charge to another person. The imputation of Adam's sin to us means that we are charged with it and therefore suffer the consequences of it. God chose Adam to be our representative, and as R.C. Sproul states, "At no time in all of human history have we been more accurately represented than in the Garden of Eden."[2] We are not sinners because we sin. We sin because we are sinners.

The Second Imputation: Our Guilt to Christ

I'm sure I've raised questions in your mind I don't have space to answer here. Like most of the doctrines presented in this book, you would do well to study this one in greater detail for the rest of your life. A common objection to this doctrine is that it is not fair that we should suffer for a wrong someone else has done. That objection assumes that if we had been in Adam's place, we would have done something totally different. We would have perfectly obeyed. Aside from that unlikely scenario, it is logically inconsistent for a Christian to argue against the first imputation while at the same time to firmly believe in the second. If the first imputation is not fair, neither is the second.

In the second imputation, our sin is imputed, or transferred, to Christ when we put our faith in him alone. I know of no Christian who has trouble with this doctrine. We all find comfort in the fact that "the Lord has laid on him the iniquity of us all" (Isa 53:6). "For our sake," writes Paul, "he made him to be sin who knew no sin, so that in him we might become the righteousness of God" (2 Cor 5:21). The parallels between Adam and Jesus (the second Adam) are clear: "Therefore, as one trespass led to condemnation for all men, so one act of righteousness leads to justification and life for all men" (Rom 5:18). By his work on the cross, Christ removed our sin from us "as far as the east is from the west" (Ps 103:12).

The Third Imputation: Christ's Righteousness to Us

God's mercy does not end with subtracting guilt from our account. He goes further to add Christ's righteousness. By removing our sin, he puts our balance at zero, but we are still broke. By adding the righteousness of his son, he makes us rich beyond measure. He not only paid our debt, but he also

2. Sproul, *Chosen by God*, 94.

made us his children, giving us full access to his palace and royal table (John 14:2–3; Ps 23:6).

Before trusting Christ, Paul was obsessed with rules, rituals, and regulations. He was relying on his own righteousness, depending on his own obedience, to justify himself in God's sight. Trusting Christ changed all that, and he stopped depending on a "righteousness of my own that comes from the law, but that which comes through faith in Christ, the righteousness from God that depends on faith" (Phil 3:9). After trusting Christ, his hope was built on an alien righteousness, a righteousness from outside of him, the imputed righteousness of Christ.

Many Christians have called this "The Great Exchange," possibly based on Martin Luther's admonition to pray "Thou Lord Jesus art my righteousness, but I am thy sin. Thou hast taken on thyself what is mine and hast given to me what is thine. Thou hast taken upon thyself what thou wast not, and hast given to me what I was not."[3]

In this unspeakably kind transaction, John Calvin declared "we cannot be condemned for our sins, from whose guilt he has absolved us, since he willed to take them on himself as if they were his own. This is the wonderful exchange which, out of his measureless benevolence, he has made with us; that, becoming Son of man with us, he has made us sons of God with him . . ."[4]

So here's a trick question: *True or False: We are saved by works.* It all depends on what you mean by works. The answer is false if the statement means we are saved by our own works. The answer is true if the statement means we are saved by Christ's works. In a way then, we are saved by works after all. We are not saved by our own works, but by the works of Christ on our behalf. His perfect obedience to all of the law of God is imputed to our account. In salvation, Christ got what I deserve and I get what he deserves. And as believers, we can forever rest in the fact that God now and forevermore accepts us for Christ's sake.

This legal standing before God is an unspeakable source of comfort for Christians. After explaining these themes in great detail in the first seven chapters of Romans, Paul joyfully announces "there is therefore now no condemnation for those who are in Christ Jesus" (Rom 8:1). Note the position of the believer: "in Christ Jesus." This prepositional phrase is extremely important in Christian doctrine and is used eighty-nine times in the New

3. Luther, "Instructions."
4. Calvin, *Institutes,* 2:1362.

Testament. Here are a few examples to give you a sense of your identity as a Christian:

> For *in Christ Jesus* you are all sons of God, through faith (Gal 3:26)

> So you also must consider yourselves dead to sin and alive to God *in Christ Jesus* (Rom 6:11)

> [Nothing] will be able to separate us from the love of God *in Christ Jesus* our Lord (Rom 8:39)

> And because of him you are *in Christ Jesus*, who became to us wisdom from God, righteousness and sanctification and redemption (1 Cor 1:30).

> For as in Adam all die, so also *in Christ* shall all be made alive (1 Cor 15:22).

> Therefore, if anyone is *in Christ*, he is a new creation. The old has passed away; behold, the new has come (2 Cor 5:17).

> There is neither Jew nor Greek, there is neither slave nor free, there is no male and female, for you are all one *in Christ Jesus* (Gal 3:28).

Being in Christ is like being in a full-body Kevlar suit. All the wrath of God aimed at your sin fell on the Son of God. In Christ, you are safe. Saved. Christian, because you are in Christ, when God looks at you, he sees Jesus.

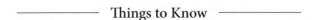

Things to Know

- What are the 3 great imputations?

— 20 —

Every Man Needs a Father

*I could no longer believe in the God of my tradition, and acknowledged that I
was an agnostic: I don't "know" if there is a God; but I think that if there is one,
he certainly isn't the one proclaimed by the Judeo-Christian tradition, the one
who is actively and powerfully involved in this world. And so I stopped going
to church.*

–BART EHRMAN, PROFESSOR OF RELIGIOUS STUDIES[1]

*The Lord's Prayer, in the plain form in which the head of the family shall teach it
to his household: Our Father who art in heaven. What does this mean? Answer:
Here God would encourage us to believe that he is truly our Father and we are
truly his children in order that we may approach him boldly and confidently in
prayer, even as beloved children approach their dear father.*

–LUTHER'S SMALL CATECHISM, 1529[2]

ON A SCALE OF 1–10, how is your relationship with your father? A ten
means that no matter your age, you feel respect for your father because he
is a credible man marked by character and competence. For that reason,
you trust him to keep your secrets and give you good advice. He has a command of sound doctrine and he leads a disciplined and self-denying life.
You know he is praying for you and you often give him specific things to
pray about. He has the guts to speak the truth to you, but you don't doubt
for a second that he loves you and would make sacrifices in your best interest. You might be fifty years old, but he is still your role model in marriage
because you have seen the way he treats your mother. You might be sitting

1. NPR, "Bart Ehrman."
2. 3:1.

on a good nest egg, but you still seek his financial counsel. You find it easy to honor your father, because he is an honorable man.

A one means that your father failed you in destructive ways. Perhaps he is an absent father and was never a part of your life. Nearly one in four children is growing up without their biological fathers[3] and the chances are good that you are one of those in that growing minority. Maybe your father was present, but you wish he had been absent. Perhaps he was (or is) emotionally or physically abusive, and you bear the scars inflicted by a weak and insecure man.

Most of our dads are somewhere in between. As we were growing up, our fathers often felt distracted, tired, guilty, overworked, and scared. They did not live up to their own expectations, let alone ours. They fell short largely because they had imperfect fathers. Yet, your father holds a peculiar power in your life. How many of our achievements are driven by the desire to impress our fathers and win their approval? God only knows. And before you blame all of your problems on this important man in your life, take note of the shortcomings of your children's father.

The longing remains. Every man knows what it is to be lonely and frightened, presenting a confident front in our marriages or in the marketplace, acting tough and bulletproof on the outside, when inside, we are fragile and easily broken. No matter how old you are, you still need to know that there is someone bigger, stronger, smarter, and better who is looking out for you, taking care of you, protecting, providing, and guiding you. Men, no matter your age, you never outgrow your need for a father.

Every Man Has Two Fathers

Ask most people if we are all God's children, and they will quickly say yes. Skin color and net worth make no difference; we are all the children of God. It doesn't matter who you are or what you've done. By virtue of being human, you are a child of God. Right? Let's look at what Jesus said.

When confronted by the religious leaders of his day, Jesus made a shocking accusation: "You are of your father, the devil" (John 8:44). They bore a striking family resemblance. Like the devil, they hated Jesus and wanted to kill him. Like the devil, they hated the truth and tried to suppress it. Like the devil, they believed and told lies about God, drawing

---

3. Of students in grades 1 through 12, 39 percent (17.7 million) live in homes absent their biological fathers. See Nord and West, "Fathers' and Mothers' Involvement," Table 1.

people away from him. For that reason, Jesus knew they were not children of God. "If God were your Father," explained Jesus, "you would love me" (John 8:42). That's the first mark of a child of God: he or she will love Jesus. Not some made-up Jesus. Not a Jesus pressed into a pre-conceived mold. Not "another Jesus" (2 Cor 11:4), revised and reworked, but the real Jesus, clearly revealed in Scripture.

It is hard to grasp the impact that Jesus' statement would have made. He was talking to deeply religious, devout, praying people, but he could not have been clearer. Unless and until someone receives Jesus as Lord and Savior, that person is a child of the devil. That means he is the legal heir of the devil and will inherit all that he has coming to him: "the eternal fire prepared for the devil and his angels" (Matt 25:41). The devil had no hand in the creation of his children since all humans are the offspring of God (Acts 17:29), but to be an offspring is not to be a legal heir, entitled to the sit at the Father's table in the Father's house, enjoying the rights and privileges of being a son or daughter.

So everyone has two fathers. First, everyone has a biological father. Your father may have been admirable, abusive, or absent, but if you are reading this, it is because you have or had, an earthly father. If your earthly father was not wise and good and brave, if he did not provide for you, protect you and teach you what you need to know to succeed, if he did not serve you by leading you and bringing loving discipline into your life, if he manipulated you with fear or guilt, if he used you for a selfish agenda, then you may be tempted to project these features onto God, thinking your heavenly Father bears these traits. Even if your earthly father was in the top ten percent of the greatest dads on earth, he fell short in more ways than you can know. He got tired, irritable, and sick. When you needed him most, he was away or asleep. Even when he wanted to do what was best for you, he frequently did not know what was best, and often when he knew what was best for you, he was powerless to do anything about it.

The world, then, is divided in two. Everyone has an earthly father, but those who love Jesus have a heavenly Father and will inherit eternal life. Those who hate Jesus, who do not believe his claims and trust him alone for salvation, have the devil as a father and will inherit death and destruction.

So how does one become a child of God? The apostle John is clear: "But to all who did receive him, who believed in his name, he gave the right to become children of God" (John 1:12). When we are justified by faith alone, we are adopted into the family of God, and "receive the spirit of adoption as sons, by whom we cry out, "Abba! Father!" (Rom 8:15).

The family of God is diverse. It doesn't matter who you are, where you are from, or what you have done. Skin color, gender, and net worth make no difference. If you know, love, obey, and exalt Jesus Christ his Son, then God is your father. In Christ, "There is neither Jew nor Greek, there is neither slave nor free, there is no male and female" (Gal 3:28). All of his children have equal access to the Father through the only mediator, Jesus Christ (1 Tim 2:5). And as unbelievable as it sounds, your heavenly Father wants to spend some quality time with you in prayer.

What is prayer? Simply put, prayer is talking to God. In chapter two, we focused on listening to God in His Word. In prayer, God listens to us. Communication between you and God doesn't flow just one way. Rather, you both take turns, speaking and listening to one another.

Two Places to Pray: Public and Private Prayer

There is a place for public prayer. When believers gather together, they should pray with each other. From the earliest days of the church, the apostles "were devoting themselves to prayer" (Acts 1:14). The earliest Christians gathered together to hear God in the "apostles' teaching" and to talk to God in "the prayers" (Acts 2:42). It is only natural for the children of God, when they are together, to talk to their Father in each other's company. So it was fitting that in the final moments that Paul had with the elders of the church at Ephesus, that "he knelt down and prayed with them all" (Acts 20:36).

The prayers do not have to be pretty. God does not require eloquence, or even precision. When your child comes home from school with tears in her eyes and she tells you how her heart was broken by the cruelty of a classmate, you don't correct her grammar. Sometimes we don't know how to word our prayers. Sometimes we don't know how to say what is on our heart or even what to ask. We don't have to be nervous or anxious. We don't have to rehearse or practice. He is our Father, and he understands what we mean, even if we do not say it exactly right.

Of course, if you are leading God's people in public worship, it is wise to pray about your prayer, to ask God in private to help you lead others in a public prayer. It can be an act of love to think ahead about how you will pray in public. God, who knows your heart, will understand what you mean, but if you are not careful, your brothers and sisters may not understand what you say.

We are naturally prone to give more weight to the opinions of other people than to the opinion of God. It should be enough for us to know that God is pleased, but we are inclined "to please man" (1 Thess 2:4). So in our public prayers, we often find ourselves wondering what others think of our speaking ability. Are they impressed with our Bible knowledge? Did they notice our earnest tone? Did they pick up on our spiritual depth? Fear of such peer-review may even keep a Christian from praying publicly at all. While others may interpret his silence as humility, it is really his pride that keeps a man from praying aloud. His fear of not saying the right words reveals he is more concerned with pleasing man than God.

Those who become skilled at public prayer might become addicted to the attention it brings them. Jesus warned his disciples of this corroding influence on our prayer life. "And when you pray, you must not be like the hypocrites. For they love to stand and pray in the synagogues and at the street corners, that they may be seen by others" (Matt 6:5). By referencing synagogues, Jesus aims his criticism at his own countrymen, the Jews. However, they are not alone. Gentiles also "heap up empty phrases" in their prayers, thinking that "they will be heard for their many words" (Matt 6:7). In fact, long public prayers can be a smokescreen, a pretense (Mark 12:40), giving the appearance that the one praying is in right relationship with God when in fact, he is not.

The answer is not to avoid praying publicly, but to increase praying privately. The answer is not less time talking to your father with others present. The answer is more time talking to your father when you are alone. In fact, as you search the gospels for a record of Jesus' public prayer, you have to look very hard, but it is easy to find abundant examples of Jesus praying alone. "And after he had dismissed the crowds," we are told, then Jesus "went up on the mountain by himself to pray" (Matt 14:23). In fact, it was Jesus' custom to "withdraw to desolate places and pray" (Luke 5:16). He did most of his praying away from the crowds, and so should we.

Specifically, Jesus said to his disciples, "when you pray, go into your room and shut the door and pray to your Father who is in secret. And your father who sees in secret will reward you" (Matt 6:6). The Greek word for "secret" here is where we get the word "crypt." Can you think of anywhere more private? In the quiet places, away from people who can hear your prayers, it is just you and God. Ulterior motives are removed.

People-pleasing performances fall away. Frantic distractions are eliminated. In the secret places, we are drawn most closely to God, our Father.

How does this happen? Secrets breed intimacy. Think how we have been drawn in closer when someone looks around and whispers, "Let me tell you a secret." When people trust us enough to share personal dreams for the future or poignant regret for the past, we lean in toward them. When we reciprocate, confident they will not use this delicate information to hurt us, the relationship goes to another level. And when they use the information we share to help and encourage us, the bond is strengthened even more. That is why a healthy marriage is the most intimate human relationship of all. Husband and wife are naked and "not ashamed" (Gen 2:25), physically and emotionally. My wife knows things about me I will tell no one else. She knows more of my fears and hopes than any person on earth. Secrets breed intimacy, but my wife does not know all of my fears and hopes.

Some of my fears shame me and some of my hopes embarrass me. I have not yet reached a point that I can share everything with her, partly because I'm not sure that she would understand and partly because I think she would understand but she already bears too many burdens and partly because I am uncertain how she would respond if she actually knew everything about me. I trust my wife more than anyone on earth, and she has kept my secrets for over a quarter of a century now, yet I still hesitate to bring her every concern, every proud sin, every anxious thought, every secret aspiration.

There is one who understands, who sees the most secret places of my heart. He is my heavenly Father. He knows my aspirations and failures. He knows when I do the right things for the wrong reasons. He knows my deep regret for past sins. He knows how weak I am in saying "no" to temptations. He knows my fears about money, and looking foolish, and growing old without making much impact. He knows the people I envy and the people who intimidate me. He knows everything about me, so when I talk to him about these things in the secret places, without an audience of people I want to impress, I am not educating him. These are things he already knew. And still, my father loves me.

Your earthly father failed you somehow. And in countless ways, you will fail your children. Your father may not have known as much as you do right now. He never had the opportunities to learn about God like you have, and now you are responsible for what you know. When you are old, will your children seek your advice? Will they find in you a good role model?

Will they trust you? View you as credible man? If that happens, it will not be without much prayer. Where do you begin? As we will see, Jesus gives us a framework in the Lord's Prayer. Learn it yourself, then teach it to your kids. Pray through it alone in secret places, then gather your family and pray through it together. A lot.

—————— Things to Know ——————

- Where are the 2 places to pray?

21

Three Things God Seeks

I'm not Buddhist, I'm not Hindu, I'm not Christian, but I still feel like I have a
deep connection with God. I pray all the time—for self-control, for humility.

–KATY PERRY, SINGER[1]

Our Father in heaven,
Hallowed be Your name.
Your kingdom come.
Your will be done, on earth as it is in heaven.
Give us this day our daily bread.
And forgive us our debts, as we forgive our debtors.
And do not lead us into temptation,
But deliver us from the evil one.
For Yours is the kingdom and the power and the glory forever.
Amen.

–THE LORD'S PRAYER, MATTHEW 6:9–13[2]

IT IS GOOD TO memorize the Lord's Prayer, found in Matthew 6:9–13, because it is the Word of God and the more of God's Word we commit to
memory, the better. I also think that it is good to recite the Lord's Prayer,
either alone or with other believers. Doing so at the side of an open grave
with other believers has often brought me much comfort; however, the danger of reciting the Lord's Prayer is that it can lead to the very thing Jesus

1. Hoffman, "Katy Conquers All."

2. While all other Scripture references in this book are from the English Standard
Version, I have chosen to use the New King James Version for the Lord's Prayer because
many, if not most, Christians in North America who have memorized it, memorized it
in a version closer to this one.

prohibited: "do not heap up empty phrases" thinking that you will be heard for your "many words" (Matt 6:7).

It is tempting to go through the motions, mechanically repeating familiar words that don't reflect the true condition of our hearts, but reciting the Lord's Prayer will only be meaningless if you let it be. In the same way, singing *Amazing Grace*, which you may have sung a thousand times before, will only be meaningless if you let it be. The greatest value of the Lord's Prayer is that it gives us a framework of how our time alone with God should go. John Calvin insisted that it was not the intention of Jesus to limit our prayers only to the prescribed words of the Lord's Prayer, but that we should use it to "frame our prayers."[3] It is a model to follow that gives us examples of the kinds of things God wants us to talk about when we talk to him. Specifically, the prayer is divided into six petitions. Here are the first three.

1. "Hallowed be your name": Father, make yourself famous in all the earth!

Chances are good you haven't used the word "hallowed" in a while. The closest you may have come was last October at Halloween. You can trace both words back to the same word, which means "to make holy." To make holy is to set something or someone apart, to distinguish it or them from all others. Of all the names of all the imagined gods in all of history, our Father's name is above all other names. He alone is "the true God; he is the living God and the Everlasting King" (Jer 10:10). Our Father is God, "there is no other besides him" (Deut 4:35). There are still millions who have not heard his name.

Then there are millions who have heard his name, but dare to "mock the living God" (2 Kgs 19:16). They do not treat his name with the respect and honor it deserves. They have not set it apart and made it holy. From the beginning of human history, people have worshipped false, dead, non-existent gods "formed by the art and imagination of man" (Acts 17:29). Still today, "all the gods of the peoples are worthless idols, but the Lord made the heavens" (Ps 96:5). Strong hope in false gods is a false hope that leads to a tragic end. As devout and passionate and sincere as they might appear to be, religious people all over the globe "keep on praying to a god that cannot save" (Isa 45:20).

3. Calvin, *Commentaries*, 16:316.

Only the true and living God, the Creator of heaven and earth, can save. Only he can rescue us from our sin. That's one of the reasons Jesus gave us the Great Commission. He commands us to make disciples of all nations (Matt 28:18–20) because that is their only hope. They must hear and revere the name of our Father.

What is the Father's name? Does this mean the people of the world have to merely hear the word "God" or "Lord" or "Lord God Almighty" or "the Most High God" or "the Everlasting God" or the several other names by which God is addressed in the Bible? If so, which name? The Lord's Prayer says "your name," not "your names." Is there one name in particular the world must hear?

Perhaps this question can be resolved when we understand that "name" can mean "reputation." Even today we speak of someone who has a good reputation as having a "good name." The psalmist declares, "Your name, O Lord, endures forever, your renown, O Lord, throughout all ages (Ps 135:13). Here, "name" and "renown" are used interchangeably. Renown refers to God's reputation and fame in the earth. So the world must not only hear God's name. They must be aware of God's fame. They must hear about what he has done and said, his works and his words. For example, the world needs to hear about the things you have read about in this book. People need to hear that he is the Creator and Redeemer who has revealed himself in Scripture. They need to hear the truths of the Apostles' Creed, the legal demands of the Ten Commandments, and the free grace of the gospel. These are things for which God is famous.

And since the pinnacle of God's remarkable deeds is the incarnation, they need to hear how God came near to us in human flesh. It is impossible to hallow God's name apart from knowing, loving, obeying, and exalting Jesus Christ. It is impossible to call God your Father without receiving his Son.

So when we ask God to make his name hallowed, we are asking him to cause the message of the Bible to spread to places on the planet where they have no Bible. We are asking God to send out missionaries, not only to our community, but to the entire world, missionaries who will tell people about Jesus. We are asking God to plant churches in cities where there is no church to bear witness to his grace. We are asking God to make himself famous in all the earth so that everyone knows what he has said and done.

Not only that, we are asking that people will believe and receive what they hear about God's reputation. We are asking God to change their hearts so that they repent, surrender, and bend their knee in submission to Christ.

We are asking God to cause them to revere, respect, and honor his name by turning to Christ alone for their salvation. We are asking God to glorify himself by empowering these believers to live good lives and do good works that enhance the reputation, the name, of their heavenly father (Matt 5:16).

When we ask God to make his name hallowed, we are asking him to cause people everywhere to worship him alone as Sovereign God and to renounce all false gods and idols (1 Thess 1:9). We make this request because "there is salvation in no one else, for there is no other name under heaven given among men by which we must be saved" except the name of Jesus (Acts 4:12).

And importantly, we are asking God to use us to answer this request. We are offering ourselves up to him to obey the Great Commission (Matt 28:18–20), to spread the gospel, to make him more famous, not only by articulating and defending our faith in Christ, but by living holy lives that reflect well on our Father's reputation. If we are not willing to be the answer to this prayer, we are being disingenuous when we pray it.

2. "Your Kingdom come": Father, continue to build the church and capture more territory!

After Rome was sacked by pagans in AD 410, the great bishop and theologian Augustine wrote to despairing Christians in the Roman Empire. He wanted them to know that even though Rome was falling apart, the church was not. There are two kingdoms, he explained, the kingdom of man and the kingdom of God. The kingdom of man is motivated by love for self that leads to division, bickering, and war. The kingdom of God is motivated by love for God that leads to unity, harmony, and peace. The kingdom of man is temporary and will eventually disappear. The kingdom of God is permanent and will eventually conquer every square inch of the earth. The kingdom of man expands and defends its borders by coercion and physical force. The kingdom of God expands and defends it borders by prayer, acts of loving service, and persuasive preaching of the word of God. The kingdom of man is ruled by puny presidents, prime ministers, kings, and dictators who come and go. The kingdom of God is permanently ruled by Jesus Christ, the eternal King of kings. The kingdom of man we call the state. The kingdom of God we call the church.

Jesus told Peter, "I will build my church, and the gates of hell shall not prevail against it" (Matt 16:18). Nothing will stand in the way of God building his church. The head of the church is Jesus and all who come into his kingdom must come on his terms. This is no democracy, and Jesus is not running for election. He does not conduct opinion polls or bend to focus groups. His law is the "royal law" (Jas 2:8) and it is not subject to debate or open to amendments. His people do not vote or veto. Rather, they gladly, humbly, simply obey him. As their sovereign king, he will lead them wisely, provide for them fully, and protect them strongly. His kingdom is not bound by geographical borders. Christ does not rule over a theocratic "Christian Nation." Rather, Christ rules in the hearts of men and women, boys and girls, who humbly receive him and come together in community with fellow citizens to worship him. King Jesus has his people everywhere, strategically scattered among the nations of the earth. Wherever there is a church, God's kingdom has come.

As citizens of the kingdom of God spread the good news of the king's coming there will be two reactions. Some will receive him as their king, accept the terms of unconditional surrender, bow their knee in submission to him, and report for duty. These are his true disciples, believers who become the adopted children of God and citizens of the kingdom. Many more, though, will reject him as their king, rudely dismissing the terms of surrender, and stiffening their necks in defiance against him. These will be separated from his love and protection forever.

Eventually, the whole world will see him for who he is. You can bow to him now as a child of God or you can bow to him later as a defeated foe, but sooner or later, you will bow to him (Phil 2:10). Christ is head of the church, which is "a holy nation" (1 Pet 2:9). And this kingdom will continue its advance; the church will continue to grow, until its final victory over all of Christ's enemies.

It would be wrong to think that Christ is not head over the state as well. All authority has been given to Jesus (Matt 28:18) and his sovereignty extends over all creation. As sovereign God, he "rules the kingdom of men and gives it to whom he will" (Dan 4:25). "He removes kings and sets up kings" (Dan 2:21). Every presidential election only reveals whom God elects. Every king is installed by God. "His kingdom endures from generation to generation; all the inhabitants of the earth are accounted as nothing, and he does according to his will . . . none can stay his hand or say to him, 'What have you done?'" (Dan 4:35).

In providing human governments, with all of their faults and corruption, God is showing kindness to all people. In a display of common grace,

God sets up governments to restrain evil, punish the guilty, and protect the weak. Even when government officials fail to acknowledge it, all of their authority comes from God, every office is appointed by God, and officials are merely the servants of God. They are the instruments of God for the good of all citizens so that criminals will be afraid to commit crimes. Therefore, if government officials abuse their office, receive bribes, show partiality in judgment, or unjustly serve themselves rather than the people they govern, God will hold them accountable (Rom 13:1–5; John 19:11).

As disciples of Jesus, then, we hold a dual-citizenship. Christians should submit to authorities in the kingdom of man, show respect, and pay taxes (Rom 13:6). We are to pray for its success while working for its peace and prosperity (Jer 29:7). We are to shrewdly negotiate the razor's edge of submitting to earthly governments while serving the King of kings (Matt 10:16). There will be times when these two kingdoms will be in conflict and we must remember our highest allegiance is to Christ since he is "King of kings and Lord of lords" (1 Tim 6:15). Sadly, we may be put in the position of defying the state in order to obey God (Acts 5:29–30).

When Jesus teaches us to pray for God's kingdom to come, he is distinguishing the kingdom of God from the kingdom of man. *Your* kingdom, Father. We want *your* kingdom to come. We are asking God for the gospel to advance, for missionaries to cross cultures and bear fruit, for people who are now the enemies of Christ to surrender and serve him. In making this request, writes Calvin, we are expressing our "daily desire that God gather churches unto himself from all parts of the earth, that he spread and increase them in number, that he adorn them with gifts, that he establish a lawful order among them."[4]

As more and more people follow Christ, they will have a remarkable influence on whole cultures and nations. As the "salt of the earth" (Matt 5:13), more true Christians in the world will result in more restraining of corruption in the world. More Christians will become involved in the arts, entertainment, education, medicine, sports, and politics. Consequently, the more humane and compassionate the world will be. As the true church grows, evil and injustice will shrink, while divorce, crime, and poverty rates decline. In this petition, we are asking God to shape the citizens of his kingdom so that they are obvious assets to the kingdom of man, loving all people, serving the poor, creating jobs, upholding justice, and speaking truth to power. We are asking God for his kingdom to have such great

---

4. Calvin, *Institutes*, 2:905–06.

influence on the kingdom of man, on the governments of nations, that the state begins to mirror the love, justice, and compassion that is (or should be) demonstrated in the church.

While we ask for these things, we recognize that the kingdom of man is and will be in conflict with the kingdom of God until Christ returns. The kingdom of God was inaugurated at Christ's first coming but will be consummated in his second coming. When David was anointed as king by Samuel (1 Sam 16:13), he still had many years of struggle and conflict before his coronation when he was recognized as king by all of Israel.

Likewise, God anointed and presented his son as king at his baptism (Matt 3:16–17), but centuries of struggle would lie ahead of King Jesus and his loyal subjects before he is finally recognized as king by the whole world. When the king returns, the matter will be indisputably settled. Because this is true, we can say that in one sense, the kingdom is already here, but in another sense it is not yet here. It has been initiated but it has not yet been consummated. This "already/not yet" aspect of the kingdom of God means that this petition is still as relevant today as it was in Jesus' day.

That is why the citizens of the kingdom of God look forward to that final day, "waiting and hastening the coming of the day of God" (2 Pet 3:12). So when we ask our Father for his kingdom to come, we are also asking him to hasten that day when Christ returns. Interestingly, the last prayer of the Bible is a variation of this second petition: "Come, Lord Jesus!" (Rev 22:20).

Finally, in the second petition, we are asking God to rule and reign in our own hearts. We are once again bowing before him in humble submission, acknowledging his royal right to hand down his decrees and our obligation as his loyal subjects to obey them. We are entrusting ourselves to his protection and provision. We are asking him to have his way in our families and our churches, to stamp out any rebellion that would shame his name (1 Cor 5:12–13). We are asking him to use us in his army, courageously defending and boldly expanding the borders of his kingdom, recalling Peter's admonition: "In your hearts honor Christ the Lord as holy, always being prepared to make a defense to anyone who asks you for a reason for the hope that is in you; yet do it with gentleness and respect" (1 Pet 3:15).

3. "Your will be done": Father, help us all to live in a way that pleases you!

What is God's will? God's will is what he intends, what he determines, what he desires, what he wants. For centuries, followers of Christ have noticed that the Bible speaks of God's will in two ways. God's revealed will is what God has chosen to communicate to us. God's secret will refers to that which God has kept hidden from us for his own reasons. "The secret things belong to the Lord our God, but the things that are revealed belong to us and to our children forever" (Deut 29:29).

We are not responsible to act on God's secret will. He will reveal what he wants us to know in due time. We are responsible to act on the revealed will of God because it contains the moral commands and instructions of God. Therefore, the revealed will of God is sometimes called the *moral will* of God and it is recorded for us in the Bible. For example, in the Bible, God reveals that if your child is a Christian, his will is for your child, if he or she marries, to marry a Christian. That is the revealed will of God (2 Cor 6:14), but the Bible does not reveal which Christian he or she should marry. He will bring someone into your child's life at the right time. You do not know who this will be or when it will happen, but God does. That is God's secret will. Likewise, the Bible reveals that it is God's will that you obey the Great Commission and do your part to make disciples of all nations. It does not reveal where you should obey this command, whether here in the United States or in China.

In this, the third petition of the Lord's Prayer, the focus is on the revealed will, or the moral will, of God. Here we are asking God to do several things.

First, we are asking God to cause the Bible to be translated, published, distributed, read, proclaimed, explained, and obeyed all over the world (Rom.12:2; Col 1:9; 1 Thess 4:13; Rom 10:13–17). To do God's will is to obey God, to do what God wants. How do you know what God wants? We don't have to guess, speculate, or assume. God's will is revealed in his Word.

For example, suppose your daughter tells you she wants to move in and share a bed with her boyfriend. Among the many good reasons you could give her for not moving in with her boyfriend is this: It is not God's will! She doesn't even have to pray about it! How does she know God's will in this matter? He has revealed it in his word: "For this is the will of God, your sanctification: that you abstain from sexual immorality" (1 Thess 4:3–4). So when you pray the third petition, you are asking God to convince your daughter that this is true, convict her that it is good, and enable her to obey it.

Second, in this petition we are asking God to enable people to do the hard and disciplined work of interpreting the Bible accurately (Eph 5:17; Heb 13:21; 2 Tim 3:16–17; Eph. 4:11). Just because people have a Bible doesn't mean they know the truth. From the beginning, the enemy has been twisting God's word. In the garden, Adam and Eve had God's Word, but Satan doubted, distorted, and misquoted it. When this happens today, people do not know God's will and as a result, do not do God's will. For that reason, we must pray that people will "understand what the will of the Lord is" (Eph 5:17).

Everyone approaches the Bible with bias and prejudice. We have our own will. We want to do what we want to do. So we are inclined to find ways to enlist the Bible to accommodate our will. We misquote the Bible. We dilute and downplay what it says. Or we may simply delete large parts of it, ignoring difficult passages and pretending whole swaths of Scripture are not even there. We treat the Bible like a salad bar from which we pick and choose according to personal tastes. We can only overcome our bias with the Father's help. Only by grace can we say "not my will, but yours be done" (Luke 22:42).

Third, in this petition we are asking God to empower us to choose his will, even if it is difficult and results in suffering (1 Thess 5:18; Heb 10:36; 1 Pet 3:17; 4:19; Luke 22:42). Most of us can relate to Mark Twain who famously quipped, "It ain't those parts of the Bible that I can't understand that bother me, it is the parts that I do understand."[5] So notice that we are not asking the Father, "your will be *known*." We are asking him: "your will be *done*." We must make this request with a heart of submission. We are saying, "Lord, I'm not sure what I will find here in your Word today, but whatever it is, whether I like it or not, whether it is easy or hard, whether it fits my preconceived notions or blows them away, I will do it. You are my Father and I am your son."

Fourth, in this petition we are asking God to send his Son to consummate his kingdom on the earth (Phil 3:20; 2 Tim 4:1–4; 1 Pet 4:5). Until Jesus returns, we will be in this battle with ourselves.

I can be my own enemy. My will is the main opponent to God's will, and too often I choose mine over his. This battle rages in every human heart, but when Christ returns he will squash all rebellion and stamp out all

5. Twain, *Wit and Wisdom*, 24.

THREE THINGS GOD SEEKS

defiance. Those of us who are his children will be transformed so that our will shall always and only be perfectly in line with his will. Finally, the will of God shall be done on earth exactly as it is done in heaven.

--------- Things to Know ---------

- What are the first 3 petitions of the Lord's Prayer?

22

Three Things Men Worry About

I believe in Jesus, I believe in God, I'm very spiritual, I pray.

–LADY GAGA, RECORDING ARTIST[1]

Question 116: . . . we rest assured that, in spite of our unworthiness, he will certainly hear our prayer for the sake of Christ our Lord as he has promised us in his word.

–THE HEIDELBERG CATECHISM, 1563

EVERY MAN I KNOW wants to be stronger than he is. No man aspires to weakness. We admire men who are physically strong, who can push harder, run faster, jump higher, and lift more than the average man. When we are young men, our bodies seem to get stronger every day. Testosterone levels rise and muscle mass grows. We surpass the strength of our mothers and sisters, and then, elated, we eventually surpass the strength of our own fathers to discover this truth: "The glory of young men is their strength, but the splendor of old men is their gray hair" (Prov 20:29). Unfortunately for me (and men like me) when I finally got old enough for my hair to turn gray, it turned loose.

Testosterone levels peak in our early thirties where we reach our physical prime. From that point on, strength-wise, it's downhill. This is when we start to see professional athletes retire from their careers. It is rare to find wide receivers in the NFL and power forwards in the NBA over forty. Sadly, they are no longer strong enough to do their work. Their bodies have failed them. Their strength has waned.

For the rest of us, who are mere mortals, our work is not as physically demanding. Yet each job still requires some degree of physical strength. In

1. Amelia, "Katy Perry, Lady Gaga."

addition, every man's job also requires certain levels of intellectual strength, brainpower. To make a living, a man has to be strong enough to go to work, and smart enough to know what to do once he gets there. In addition, he must be emotionally strong, able to manage his passions, be steady and reliable, like a rock. If we don't, we will do or say things that will get us fired.

It is no surprise, then, that we tend to associate manliness with strength. Strong bodies and minds can put us in a strong financial positions and help us fulfill our calling to strongly protect and provide for our families. Every man secretly yearns for his wife to admire him and believe in her heart that he is strong enough to protect her and smart enough to provide for her. That's why, when a man loses his health or his job, he often feels like he has lost his identity as a man. He feels weak and impotent. And no man wants that.

Along the way, a man harbors great fears that he will be found out. He is not as strong as others might think. He may hide his fears in boasting, buying status symbols, or seeking pleasure, but deep down, he is afraid. Then a marriage crisis, an ethical breach, a health issue, a career setback, or inevitable aging unsettles him, chips away at his confidence, reveals how weak he is. All men are insecure, though some are better than others at hiding it.

So he secretly worries. He may not publicly admit his weakness, but he privately frets about it. He worries and he wonders about three questions: *Am I strong enough to provide for my family? Am I strong enough to confess my failures? Am I strong enough to resist temptation?*

While the first three petitions of the Lord's Prayer focus on our Father (his name, his kingdom, his will) the last three petitions focus on his children (our bread, our sins, our temptation). The first three focus on what we can do for God, while the second three focus on what God can do for us.

4. "Give us this day, our daily bread": Father, give us all we need to do your will on earth.

Men worry about money. They know, deep down, they are called to be bread-winners who provide for their families. So credible men get up early, go to their jobs, do good work, and bring home money. Providing for his family is an honorable calling and when a man rejects it he is held in disgrace. Paul reminded the Thessalonians that when he was with them, he didn't "eat anyone's bread without paying for it, but with toil and labor" he worked hard so as not to be a financial burden to anyone (2 Thess 3:8).

Unfortunately, some in the church refused to work, expecting others to meet their needs, but Paul commanded the church: "If anyone is not willing to work, let him not eat" (2 Thess 3:10). Men are to "do their work quietly and to earn their own living" (2 Thess 3:12). A thief who comes to Christ is required to renounce his former life and get a job, "doing honest work with his own hands, so that he may have something to share with anyone in need" (Eph 4:28). Yet even though a man works hard, if he is wise he will always acknowledge that it is God who "supplies seed to the sower and bread for food" (2 Cor 9:10). Only by God's grace is a man strong enough to go to work and smart enough to do his work. Only by God's grace does he have a job. All daily bread is a gift from his Father.

Each day, a Christian man must remind himself of this truth, because some days it is hard to trust God. On those days, a man tends to worry and doubt. Am I strong enough to provide for my family and myself? Do I have enough money? Do I make enough money? Have I saved enough money? Can I keep this job? Can I get a job? Will I get a promotion? Should I ask for a raise? What will the economy do? Will I be able to retire?

In the fourth petition, we are asking God to provide us with enough daily calories to live and work for him. It is related to the third petition in that you can't do God's will on earth if you don't live on earth, and you can't live on earth if you starve to death. So we are asking God to give us what we need to live and have the energy to do his will.

In making this request we are asking God to humble us with the knowledge that he owns everything and we own nothing. God never asks us for anything because he has need of nothing and we have nothing he needs. He commands us to give and never asks. We ask him to give and never command (Exod 19:5; John 19:11; 1Cor 10:26).

Every good thing we have is a gift from him. Bread represents all of our material needs for living on this earth, but we deserve none of it (1 Tim 4:4; Jas 1:17). For that reason, this petition is also a plea for God to cause us to be more grateful and give him thanks for all of these good gifts. It is proper for you to lead your family to bow their heads at the dinner table and give thanks to God. It is fitting to pray before and after surgeries and thank God for doctors, hospitals, medicine, and healing (Phil 4:6; 1 Tim 4:3; Matt 15:36; 26:27).

This petition also involves a request to God to enable us to discern between "wants" and "needs," between luxuries and necessities. Notice it is "daily" bread. The obesity problem in America is largely due to eating tomorrow's bread along with today's. Notice also it is daily "bread," not filet mignon. It is not wrong to eat filet mignon, but it is probably wrong to eat it daily. So in this request, we are asking the Lord to keep our lives simple. Instead of cluttering our worlds with gadgets, gizmos, toys, and amusements that distract us from him, we are asking him to give us only what we need to serve him well (1 Tim 6:8; Heb 13:5; Luke 3:14; Phil 4:11).

Also inherent in this petition is a humble request for a good job. How do you get bread? You buy it with money. How do you get money? You earn it. Normally, the way God provides us with daily bread is through hard work and honest labor. By extension, we are also asking the Lord to bless our business or practice so we can provide daily bread for others by creating jobs for those who can work and giving to those who cannot (2 Thess 3:10; 2 Cor 9:7; 1 Tim 5:8).

While unbelievers will be constantly worried about these things, a Christian man will find peace in the promise of Jesus: "But seek first the kingdom of God and his righteousness, and all these things will be added to you" (Matt 6:33). Instead of frantically worrying about money, he will give his children a good example of praying about money and his daily bread, and publicly giving thanks for God's provision (Phil 4:6–7).

5. "Forgive us our debts": Father, delete ours sins so we can enjoy you.

Men generally hate to admit when they are wrong. We feel pressure to project an image of strength, but confessing guilt is a sign of weakness. Right?

Actually, the opposite is true. Cowards deny responsibility, shift blame, and lie to avoid the consequences of their decision. It is the mark of weakness to pretend and pose and dodge our duty.

When the first man committed the first sin, his first response was an act of weakness in which he blamed his wife (Gen 3:12). We've been blaming our wives, and everyone else, ever since. Instead of strongly standing up and taking responsibility for our weaknesses and failures, we often slink away and evade responsibility for what we have done. It takes a strong man to admit he is weak.

In the fifth petition, we humbly acknowledge that we owe God our worship, thanks, and perfect obedience. Yet none of us have given him all we owe and that puts us in debt. We are in more debt than we can grasp because we have not only done what he did not want us to do, but we have not done what he wanted us to do. Some of our sin was deliberate and some unintentional, some premeditated, and some spontaneous. We are unable to pay this exorbitant debt and the penalty for non-payment is physical, spiritual, and eternal death (Rom 6:23).

Remember, this prayer is for the children of God who can call God their Father. As we have seen, Jesus came to pay that debt for us (Col 2:13–14) and therefore, if we trust in Christ, our sins are already forgiven; the debt has been paid in full on the cross. If that is the case, why are we taught to ask God to forgive us?

It might help to think of it like this. When we first trusted Christ, we confessed our sin and asked God to forgive us for Christ's sake. At that point, God adopted us into his family so that we can call him our Father. We initially asked God to forgive us in order to establish a relationship with him. That relationship will remain forever. If you are a child of God, you will always be a child of God (John 10:28–29). You are eternally secure.

That security doesn't mean you stop sinning. Even as a child of God you will disobey him. So in the fifth petition we are instructed to ask God to forgive us, not to *establish* our relationship as his child, but to *enjoy* our relationship as his child. As a child of God you can disobey him, but when you do, neither of you will enjoy your relationship. To enjoy your relationship with him, you must "try to discern what is pleasing to the Lord" (Eph 5:10) and do it. And one thing that pleases the Lord is to agree with him about our sin.

In the fifth petition we are asking the Lord to show us mercy and once again demonstrate his incalculable patience with us. God loves to forgive his children who repent and return to him, so he reminds us that "if we confess our sins, he is faithful and just to forgive us our sins and to cleanse us from all unrighteousness" (1 John 1:9). Even though we are unfaithful to him every day, he is never unfaithful to us. Even though we don't deserve it, we are pleading with God to let our sin go and not hold it against us.

Each time we make this request, our attention is once again drawn to the cross of Christ. The reason the Father can forgive us is that his Son paid the debt on the cross. He forgives us only for Christ's sake. Because of what Christ has done for us, God is free to give us mercy and not justice. So in our weakness we find great strength, and in that strength, we can "with confidence draw near to the throne of grace, that we may receive mercy and find grace to help in time of need" (Heb 4:16). That strong confidence does not come from ourselves but from God. We have great confidence in what Christ has done for us.

In the fifth petition, we are also asking God to make us forgiving people. We are inviting him to change our heart so that we treat other people in our lives the way God has treated us. We are asking for his grace to love our enemies and not retaliate against those who hurt us. Weak men seek revenge. Strong men confront, speak the truth in love, and pursue reconciliation.

Does this mean that forgiving others is a condition for salvation? Are we justified by this good work of forgiving others? We know this cannot be true. Justification is by faith alone, but forgiving others will be a consequence of our salvation. We are not saved because we forgive our debtors. We forgive our debtors because we are saved. While forgiving others is not a condition for establishing our relationship as a child of God, it is a condition for enjoying our relationship as a child of God.

Men, the fact is that you and I are weak. Are you strong enough to admit it to God, your wife, your children, and each other?

6. "Lead us not into temptation": Father, protect me from future sins so I can glorify you.

When God saves a man, he puts a desire in his heart to be loyal to Christ no matter what. We swear allegiance to our Lord and King and go forth to conquer. We all resonate with Peter's manly promise to Jesus: "Even if I must die with you, I will not deny you!" (Matt 26:35). And we all know what happened next. Temptation. Weakness. Failure. A man who loves God with all his heart will find himself worrying if he is strong enough to resist the temptations that come his way.

In the sixth petition, we recognize that our failure to fight temptation affects the first three petitions. When we surrender to sin, God's name is not hallowed, God's kingdom is not advanced, and God's will is not done. In the fifth petition, Jesus teaches us to ask for forgiveness of past sins so we can enjoy him. In the sixth petition, Jesus teaches us to ask for God's help in avoiding future sins so we can glorify him.

Every time we sin, we are telling the world that no matter what we say, Jesus is not enough for us; Jesus does not satisfy us or know what is best for us. We are sending a message that we know better than Jesus and are wiser than the King of kings. In this, God is not glorified.

So in the sixth petition we ask God to deliver us from the evil one[2] as we admit that our adversary is committed to working against everything God is working for. If God is for his name being hallowed, Satan is for God's name to be unknown, disrespected, and spoken in vain. If God is for his kingdom to come and his church to grow and missionaries to be sent, then Satan is for God's kingdom to stall, his church to be divided, and missionaries to be discouraged and unsupported. We cannot protect ourselves from Satan, so we ask God to protect us.

Tests vs. Temptations

The same word for temptation here can also refer to a test. In Matthew 4:1, Jesus was led by the Spirit to be tempted by the devil. Does this mean that God tempts us to sin? No, for God "tempts no one" (Jas 1:13). So what is the difference?

Tests are designed by God and intended to strengthen and send us out to serve him. When your schoolteacher gave you a test, it was for your good. She led you into a difficult, stressful situation, but she wanted you to do well. She wanted you to succeed so she could send you to the next grade, and eventually to college and the marketplace. Tests are often unwelcome and unpleasant, but God often permits them into your life for your good.

Temptations, on the other hand, are designed by Satan and intended to weaken and trap you. Satan is trying to trip you up. He wants to weaken and wound you and keep you from making disciples and glorifying God. Men of God must be alert to every "snare of the devil" (1 Tim 3:7). Why? Because when you are caught in a trap what can you do? Nothing. What can you contribute to the battle? Nothing. Who can you help to know, love, obey, and exalt Christ? No one.

Consider the man who is trapped in an adulterous affair. What happens to his evangelistic zeal? When most of his co-workers in the office have figured out what is going on, how confident is he in sharing the gospel and exhorting them to repent from their sin and turn to Christ? How concerned

2. The definite article is used in the Greek: literally, "the evil," and most likely refers to Satan.

will he be to give generously to support missionaries when his money is tied up in motel rooms and secret trips? How much will he pray for the success of his church? Not much. He is caught in a snare and out of the fight.

Types of Temptation

There are two types of temptation. The first type is the temptation to renounce and defy Christ our king in order to escape pain. Persecution, for example, is painful, and many a man has escaped pain by denying Christ, keeping his mouth shut, or flying under the radar to avoid a hostile reaction.

There is an expression that comes from the days of sailing ships on the high seas: "Fly your true colors." Early warships often carried flags from other nations. If, for example, a French ship was in British seas, it might fly a British flag to avoid confrontation or to make a surprise attack. To fly your true colors as a Christian means you are not ashamed of the gospel, and you let people know it no matter who is with you. Peter had a chance to fly his true colors when confronted by a girl during Jesus' trial, but instead he gave in to the temptation to deny Christ in order to escape pain.

The second type of temptation is the temptation to renounce and defy Christ our King in order to gain pleasure. In the first temptation, the fruit in the garden was pleasant to the sight and a delight to the eyes (Gen 3:6). Temptation often begins with a look. We see something (or someone) beyond the boundaries God has set for us, and yet it looks good. We see, pursue, and partake, even though God has said "no," because, at least initially, it brings great pleasure.

There are at least four main areas in which we are tempted. First, *socially*, we hunger for the approval of others. This temptation appeals to our pride and leads us to comparison. When we feel superior to others spiritually, physically, intellectually, or racially, we are easily intoxicated by the praise and applause of the world. Longing to be popular, praised, worshipped, and idolized by other creatures, we make lifestyle decisions based on how we will be perceived by the public, without regard for God's opinion (1 Pet 4:19; 1 Thess 2:4; Gal 1:10; Matt 10:28).

Second, *financially*, we are prone to love money more than God. If you ever wonder whether or not you love money, ask yourself this question. What are you willing to do to get it and keep it? Are you willing to lie to a customer? Cheat a partner? Underreport to the IRS? Steal from an employer? Fail to disclose deficiencies in the car you are selling? Are you willing to rob God by refusing to give generously to his work and workers? Are you willing to live in luxury but ignore the needs of the poor? Are you willing to neglect church attendance in order to make more money? In other words, are you willing to sin against God in order to get and keep more money? Then you love money and you have fallen to temptation.

Third, *sexually*, men in particular are vulnerable to temptation. Most men have a significant appetite for sex, and many a man has fallen into this trap. In thirty years of pastoring, I've seen a lot of smart men do stupid things. King David usually comes to mind when we think of sexual temptation. He was in the wrong place at the wrong time, saw an attractive woman showing too much skin, and abused his power to get her in bed—and his life and ministry were never the same after that. Though he sought and received forgiveness, the consequences of his moral weakness plagued him and his family for the rest of his life.

In contrast, Joseph was persistently pursued by a married woman in a way that most men dream of. How many of us could resist the delicious invitation from a seductive woman, "Lie with me?" Only the strongest men can say, "How then can I do this great wickedness and sin against God?" (Gen 39:9). Whether the woman speaks from an empty house or a computer screen, only God can strengthen us to say "no."

Fourth, *doctrinally*, we are constantly tempted to distort Scripture in order to rationalize our treason against God. Since we are naturally inclined to love popularity, sex, and money, we want to find loopholes in the Bible. The enemy's favorite strategy is to twist Scripture, misquoting it, misusing it, misinterpreting it, and misapplying it. In the first temptation, he places doubt in Eve's mind: "Did God actually say, 'You shall not eat of any tree in the garden?'" (Gen 3:1). In his temptation of Jesus in Matthew 4:6, Satan takes God's word out of context in his attempt to manipulate the Lord of lords. By smooth talk and flattery, false teachers tell people what they want to hear by distorting, denying, or deleting the apostles' teaching. "For the time is coming," warned Paul, "when people will not endure sound teaching, but having itching ears they will accumulate for themselves teachers to suit their own passions" (2 Tim 4:3). Weak men who have not been equipped with God's word will not have the strength to resist such teachers or the temptation to swallow to their seductive words. Weak men will be pushed around by smooth talkers.

If you live long enough, you will know what it is to be weak. I've kept a log of my 5K runs and bench press max for over twenty years. The time on the 5k is heading north and the max on my bench press is heading south at a rapid rate. Try as you might, your muscles will melt. Abs of steel will become mounds of mush. There are men at my gym who are well into retirement. I admire their discipline, but I have seen them in the locker room and I can see that this is not going to end well. Hope all you want that you will be the exception, but you too will join our wrinkled ranks. As the years pass, you will find more comfort in Paul's words, "So we do not lose heart. Though our outer self is wasting away, our inner self is being renewed day by day" (2 Cor 4:16). It is possible to become a stronger man every day: Strong enough to do all that God requires you to do. But the strength will not come without much prayer.

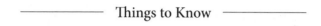

Things to Know

- What are the second 3 petitions of the Lord's Prayer?

—— 23 ——

The Fallacy of Churchless Christianity

I was the pastor of a mega-church, and lots of people came, and I did book tours and interviews and films. That's fine. But I'll take seeing God every day, which is washing dishes with my kids and walking my dog and interacting with someone I just met.

−ROB BELL, FORMER MEGA-CHURCH PASTOR[1]

The true church can be recognized if it has the following marks: The church engages in the pure preaching of the gospel; it makes use of the pure administration of the sacraments as Christ instituted them; it practices church discipline for correcting faults. In short, it governs itself according to the pure Word of God, rejecting all things contrary to it and holding Jesus Christ as the only Head. By these marks one can be assured of recognizing the true church—and no one ought to be separated from it.

−BELGIC CONFESSION, 1561

MORE AND MORE, PROFESSING Christians in America are going to church less and less. They have concluded that the church is unnecessary for a vital and warm relationship with God. When asked to explain, churchless Christians say something like this: "I want spirituality without religion." "I can do church at Starbucks while talking to another person about God." "I hate religion but I love Jesus."

So while 77 percent of Americans describe themselves as Christians,[2] millions of them will not be in church this Sunday. By one respected poll, you can count on 43 percent of Americans to attend religious services each

1. Hinch, "Where Are the People?"
2. Newport, "In U.S., 77% Identify as Christians."

week, but that's including mosques and synagogues.[3] On Easter Sunday, the highest church-attendance day of the year, almost half of all self-identified Christians will plan to do something else that day instead of publicly worshiping God.[4] Also fascinating is that 62 percent of un-churched Americans identify themselves as "Christians."[5]

What's going on here? Is it really possible to be a healthy, growing, productive, God-glorifying follower of Jesus Christ and opt out of his church? Is it legitimate to claim to be a disciple of Jesus and yet have no significant involvement in a local church?

Serving God In and Through the Local Church

When God saves us, we turn "from idols to serve the living and true God" (1 Thess 1:9). We don't serve God because he needs us in any way (Acts 17:25), but we serve him out of overflowing joy that comes from knowing, loving, obeying, and exalting him. When we love other people enough to share the gospel with them, we are "serving the Lord" (Acts 20:19). God gives us the privilege of being used by him to accomplish his sovereign purposes. God first serves us through the church as we are brought to Christ and taught to follow him, being equipped by other church members to serve in his name (Eph 4:12). Then we learn to serve God *in* the church as we find our place and function in the body of Christ (Rom 12:4). And then we serve God *through* the church as we do our part to send the gospel and missionaries to the nations (Acts 15:3). There is no consideration in all of Scripture that we might serve God by ourselves, apart from significant involvement in the local church.

The Marks of a True Believer

No one is a Christian because he says he is. That's why polls can be deceiving. Pollsters may ask people if they identify themselves as Christians, but claims call for evidence. If you say you are a Christian, you have to prove it. Paul reminds us that "if anyone is in Christ, he is a new creation. The old has passed away. Behold the new has come" (2 Cor 5:17). When God

3. Newport, "Americans' Church Attendance."
4. Rankin, "Survey: One in Five."
5. Barna Group. "Spirituality May Be Hot."

saves a man, he changes a man, and that man will "bear fruit in keeping with repentance" (Matt 3:8). One of the things that God changes is your relationship with the church.

Before coming to Christ, you are an "outsider" (1 Cor 12:24) because you are outside of the church. Since God is not yet your Father, you are not in his family, but when you are joined to Christ, you are adopted as a child of God and the church, his family, becomes your family. Being a "member of the household of God" takes priority over all other affiliations (John 1:12; Eph 2:19). If a man is not willing to put Christ above his father, mother, sister and brother, Jesus said "he cannot be my disciple" (Luke 12:46).

After Christ, your relationship with other disciples comes next. When informed that his mother and brothers had come to see him, Jesus pointed at his disciples and said, "Here are my mother and my brothers" (Matt 12:49). Because your commitment to fellow disciples now comes before all other human relationships, Jesus gave a new commandment to his followers: "A new commandment I give to you, that you love one another: just as I have loved you, you also are to love one another. By this all people will know that you are my disciples, if you have love for one another" (John 13:34–35).

How can you love other disciples if you do not meet with them? Some early Christians apparently thought they could pull that off, so they stopped coming to church, but the author of Hebrews exhorts them: "And let us consider how to stir up one another to love and good works, not neglecting to meet together, as is the habit of some, but encouraging one another, and all the more as you see the Day drawing near" (Heb 10:24–25). There are over sixty "one another/each other" commands like this in the New Testament, and there is no possible way to obey them if you are not significantly involved in a local church. How can you "bear one another's burdens" (Gal 6:2), if you don't know what another's burdens are? Therefore, it is impossible to love, obey, and exalt Jesus Christ while simultaneously and willfully remaining un-churched.

The priority we give to the church does not mean that we are to abandon our earthly families. Far from it. Our church will expect, equip, and implore us to honor our parents, love our wives, and nurture our children. However, one of the marks of a genuine believer is a sacrificial commitment to other believers in the family of God (which will make us better sons, husbands, and fathers). Jesus said to his disciples, "Whoever receives you, receives me" (Matt 10:40). So if you want Jesus, you get his church. It's a package deal. This is one of the marks of a true believer. Genuine Christians open up their lives to other disciples and meet them on the Lord's Day to publicly worship God and build up each other in love.

The 8 Meanings of the Word "Church"

The word for church used in the Greek is *ekklesia*, which literally means to be "called out." The church refers to people who have been called out by God to gather together for worship. Notice that the New Testament never uses this word to refer to a building. There are at least eight different ways that the word *church* is used in the Bible and church history.

First, the *visible church* refers to the church we can see and includes all professing Christians. With their lips, they claim to belong to Christ and with their life they give varying degrees of evidence, but we cannot see or judge the human heart. Therefore, the *visible church* includes even unbelievers who claim to know Christ, but who are not known by Christ. On the surface, they may, like Judas, give the appearance of being followers of Jesus, but in the judgment, Jesus will say, "I never knew you. Depart from me" (Matt 7:23). It is possible for even an unbeliever to say and do the things necessary to join the visible church, even though he is not a member of the invisible church.

Second, the *invisible church* refers to the church that only God can see and includes only true believers. "Man looks on the outward appearance, but the Lord looks on the heart" (1 Sam 16:7). Since "the Lord knows those who are his" (2 Tim 2:19), he is never misled by counterfeits. As he looks over the visible church each Sunday morning, he knows those in attendance who both profess and possess Christ and he knows those who profess, but do not possess, Christ. It will not be fully clear to us who is in the invisible church until Judgment Day. On that day we will know what God knows.[6]

Third, the *local church* is a group of Christians who live in the same geographic area who meet together weekly at a certain address to fulfill the purposes of the church. In this sense, there are many churches all over the world. For example, the New Testament refers to the churches in Jerusalem (Acts 8:1), Rome (Rom 16:5), Corinth (1 Cor 16:19), and Colossae (Col 4:15). This is the most common sense in which we use the word *church*.

---

6. Calvin. *Institutes*, 2:1022. "For we have said that Holy Scripture speaks of the church in two ways . . . the former church, invisible to us, is visible to the eyes of God alone . . ."

Fourth, the *universal church* refers to the assembly of the visible church that happens all over the world. In this sense, there is only one church in the world. When Jesus promised, "I will build my church" (Matt 16:18), he wasn't just referring to the church in Corinth or Ephesus. Rather he was promising to build the world-wide, universal church.

Fifth, the *militant church* refers to believers who are currently alive and engaged in the spiritual struggle against sin, the flesh, and the devil. They are still in the good fight to glorify God on earth (Eph 4:4; 6:12; 1 Tim 6:12).

Sixth, the *triumphant church* refers to those believers who have died and are currently glorifying God in heaven. They have fought the good fight and experienced triumph won for them by Jesus. When a soldier in the *militant church* dies on earth, he immediately joins the ranks of the *triumphant church* in heaven (Phil 1:21; 2 Tim 4:7–8; Eph 4:4).

Seventh, the *true church* refers to a visible church that remains faithful to the teaching of Jesus and the apostles and has the three marks of a true church (Acts 2:42; 20:27; 2 Tim 4:2; 1 Cor 11:25; Acts 2:41; 1 Cor 5:11; Matt 18:12–20).

Eighth, the *false church* refers to a visible church that never had or has departed from the central teachings of Jesus and the apostles and lacks the three marks of a true church. Having the word *church* in an organization's name does not necessarily make it a church (Acts 20:29–30; Matt 7:15–16; 24:11–24; Gal 1:6–7; 2:4; 2 Pet 2:1; Rev 2:5).

The 3 Marks of a True Church

What then are the marks of a true church? During the Reformation, the Reformers had to think through the question: When is a church not a church? Some reformers were becoming too radical and giving up on imperfect churches too soon. Instead of reforming the church, these radicals argued too quickly for separation from the church. To prevent unjustified separation, the Reformers developed three essential marks from Scripture that identify a true church.[7]

7. Calvin, *Institutes*, 2:1023. "Wherever we see the Word of God purely preached and heard, and the sacraments administered according to Christ's institution, there, it is not to be doubted, a church of God exists . . . If it has the ministry of the Word and honors it, if it has the administration of the sacraments, it deserves without doubt to be held and considered a church. For it is certain that such things are not without fruit." Here Calvin notes only two marks of a true church, but later Reformers saw a third in the second. The right administration of the sacraments can only exist if the church is well-disciplined.

The first mark is the right preaching of the Word of God. Does the church view the Bible as the final authority in all matters? Does Scripture have authority over all creeds, confessions, councils, opinions, dreams, visions, emotional experiences, liver-quivers, and individual interpretations? Does the church affirm what the apostles affirm and deny what the apostles deny? Is the Scripture respected, read, taught, and preached in all of the church's meetings? Does the church follow an intellectually honest and disciplined method of interpretation, considering what the original author intended? Does the church exhort members to honor God's Word by applying it to their lives? A true church rightly preaches the Word of God.[8]

The second mark is the right administration of the sacraments (or ordinances). Jesus gave the church only two sacraments: Baptism and the Lord's Supper. Does the church reverently preach the gospel with the picture of the death, burial, and resurrection of Christ when it baptizes new believers?[9] Does the church require baptism for membership? Does the church regularly preach the gospel in the Lord's Supper with the picture of the broken body and spilled blood of Jesus given for us? At all times does the church make clear that no one is justified by the good works of participating in the sacraments? A true church rightly administers the two sacraments.[10]

The third mark is the right practice of church discipline. Is the church well ordered and efficiently governed? Are people held accountable? Is there a way to redress grievances or bring a charge against a church leader? Are qualified church leaders vigilant to tenderly but firmly protect the church from false teaching? Are church leaders biblically discriminating on whom

---

Therefore, church discipline became for some reformers a third mark of a true church. For other reformers, church discipline was assumed to be present in the right administration of the sacraments.

8. Acts 2:42; 2 John 1:9; 2 Tim 4:1–5; 1 Cor 15:1–5; Gal 1:8–9; John 10:27; Gen 3:1–5; Matt 4:1–11; 2 Tim 2:15; Gal 1:7; 2 Pet 3:16).

9. Many churches, following most of the Reformers, also baptize the infant children of believing parents, not because they believe this "saves" the child or literally washes away sin. Rather, they believe it is a sign of the covenant which replaces the Old Testament sign of circumcision (infant baptism). Other churches that follow the Reformers on most other things, baptize only those who give a credible testimony of their belief in Christ and therefore will not baptize infants (believers' baptism only). Faithful Christians disagree on this important and significant matter. Yet all of these Christians agree that all who profess faith in Christ but have not been baptized should submit to water baptism as a matter of obedience to the Lord who commands them to be baptized.

10. Matt 28:18–20; Rom 6:4; 1 Cor 11:17–34.

the church will baptize? Are qualified church leaders diligent to protect the church from hypocrisy and scandal? Do church leaders confront, correct, and if necessary remove rebellious or divisive members from the church without partiality? Do church leaders prohibit unrepentant members from taking part in the Lord's Supper? Is there a clear way for repentant members to be restored to the church? Is the church marked by peace and unity? The true church rightly practices church discipline.[11]

The 3 Purposes of the Church

The church exists for at least three purposes.

The first purpose of the church is *exaltation*. Jesus said that God is seeking "true worshipers" (John 4:23) and gathering them into the church. God's people gather to sing "psalms and hymns and spiritual songs" (Col 3:16) and "offer to God acceptable worship, with reverence and awe" (Heb 12:28). In all of our praying, singing, Scripture reading, and delivering and listening to sermons we exalt our God who is worthy of worship.

The second purpose of the church is *education*. The Great Commission commands us to make disciples by "teaching them to observe all" that Christ commands (Matt 28:20). Therefore, teaching sound doctrine is a central purpose of the church. God gives to the church people who are specifically gifted to teach, holding official teaching positions. By their teaching they equip God's people to do ministry (Eph 4:11–13; Rom 12:7; 1 Tim 5:17). Besides that, each member teaches and admonishes one another with the Word of God. Parents teach their children, older men teach the younger men, and older women teach the younger women (Titus 2:2–4). The goal of this teaching ministry is the nurture and edification of the church so that each member matures in their faith.

The third purpose of the church is *evangelism* (to proclaim good news). The Great Commission commands us to make disciples and baptize them. Among other things, baptism is the initiation of the new believer into the church, but before he can be baptized, he must embrace the gospel. And before he can embrace the gospel, he must hear it (Rom 10:14).

Every local church is a base camp for evangelism. So God's people gather in order to worship and be equipped, and then they scatter into the world during the week as ambassadors for Christ (2 Cor 5:20). Every believer is strategically placed in his community to reach people who need to

---

11. 2 Tim 2:24; 1 Tim 3:1–13; Titus 1:5–11; 3:10–11; 1 Cor 5; Matt 18:15–20.

hear the gospel. Church members will not only tell them what it means to be a Christ-follower, but also they will show them what it means by inviting them to church. As the unbeliever observes Christians involved in *exaltation* and *education* at church, perhaps he will be convicted of his need for Christ and "falling on his face, he will worship God" (1 Cor 14:25). And then, beyond the local community, the church will sacrifice to send missionaries as ambassadors of Christ to evangelize the gospel-deprived places on our planet (Acts 13:1–3).

Fathers, Sports, and Sunday Morning

Churchless Christianity is an oxymoron in the same category with square circles, liquid ice, and gay marriage. There is no such thing. There is no way to properly know, love, obey, and exalt Christ apart from the church. We call it *the* church because it is not my church or your church. It is God's church. He loves it, with all of its faults and shortcomings, and it is precious to him because he bought it "with his own blood" (Acts 20:28).

It is in this God-ordained environment that God has called you to raise your children "in the discipline and instruction of the Lord" (Col 3:21). This job is too big for you. You need the help of your church if you are to lead your family well. When a man does not lead his wife and children to attend public worship of God on the Lord's Day, he is denying himself one of the main ways God wants to pour out his strengthening grace on that man and his family.

Declining church attendance is not peculiar to America. In Europe, the downward spiral began decades ago and the causes have been of great interest to both church leaders and sociologists. A report from Switzerland confirmed what we suspect: parents have the greatest influence on whether or not children become regular church attenders as adults. If both parents faithfully attended church, the children were more likely to do so, but the father's influence was disproportionately high. Researchers found that if the father does not go to church, no matter how regular the mother was in her religious practice, only one child in 50 became a regular church attender. However, "if a father attends regularly then regardless of the practice of the mother at least one child in 3 will become a regular church attender."[12]

Here in America, the results are similar. When both parents attend Sunday school, 72 percent of their children will attend Sunday School when

12. Quoted in Low, "Truth About Men and Church."

they are grown. If only the father attends, 55 percent of the children will attend as adults. If only the mother attends, only 15 percent of their children will maintain this practice. Father's have a disproportionate influence on their children regarding church attendance. With that comes a disproportionate responsibility.[13]

While church attendance on Sunday morning is declining among younger generations, sports attendance on Sunday mornings is on the upswing. Several years ago, Rick Reilly wrote a prophetic article for *Sports Illustrated* in which he observed that "God is competing more and more with Sunday sports—and losing. Especially with youth sports." Not long ago, coaches would not have considered scheduling practices or games on Sunday. Not anymore. More kids are coming to church late, leaving early, or not coming at all in order to play games. This is what Reilly calls "the upping of American youth sports. For some reason over-caffeinated parents feel they have to keep up with the Joneses. They used to do it with their cars. Now they do it with their kids. Upping means putting little Justin into not one soccer league but three, not one soccer camp but four."[14] Consequently, a generation of Christians is being taught that going to church on Sunday is something you do if you have nothing better to do. Where will this end? I don't know, but I do know that Dads let it come to this point, and only Dads can turn it back.

─────────── Things to Know ───────────

- What are the 8 meanings of the word *church*?

- What are the 3 marks of a true church?

- What are the 2 sacraments (or ordinances) of the church?

- What are the 3 purposes of the church?

13. Bruce and Bruce, *Becoming Spiritual Soulmates,* 52.
14. Reilly, "Let us Pray."

24

Why the Church Is Full of Hypocrites

Just in terms of allocation of time resources, religion is not very efficient. There's a lot more I could be doing on a Sunday morning.

–BILL GATES[1]

And as Christ for the keeping of this church in holy and orderly communion, placeth some special men over the church, who by their office are to govern, oversee, visit, watch; so likewise for the better keeping thereof in all places, by the members, he hath given authority, and laid duty upon all, to watch over one another.

–PARTICULAR BAPTISTS, [FIRST] LONDON CONFESSION, 1644[2]

WHEN BILL GATES WAS a boy, his parents required him to attend church on Sunday. His pastor, noticing his precocious mind, challenged him to memorize Jesus' Sermon on the Mount. Rising to the challenge, he memorized Matthew 5–7 and recited it word for word.[3] As an adult, and the wealthiest person on the planet, Gates was asked by David Frost if he believed in the Sermon on the Mount. "I don't," replied Gates, "I'm not someone who goes to church on a regular basis. The specific elements of Christianity are not something I'm a huge believer in."[4]

At least Bill Gates is consistent. If he doesn't believe "the specific elements of Christianity," it's hard to see why he would go to church. There are, however, many people who don't believe or practice the central tenets of Christianity yet go to church anyway. Some of them hold positions of leadership in the church and may even use their authority to take advantage

1. Isaacson, "Real Bill Gates."
2. Article 44.
3. Lesinski, *Bill Gates*, 15.
4. Lofton, "Warren Buffet."

of others. In contrast to Gates, they are being inconsistent. Their behavior is not only dangerous for them, it is damaging to the church.

Why do they go to church? There are a variety of reasons: family tradition, cultural expectation in regions where church attendance is relatively high, social networking. Some church members are so biblically illiterate they don't even know they don't believe or live by the central tenets of Christianity. Some know, but don't care. The end result is the same: there is a perception among many unbelievers that the church is full of hypocrites. From that perception they make the unwarranted leap: Therefore, the church's message is not true.

Of course, Jesus had a lot to say about hypocrisy and it is no accident the word used in the New Testament referred to actors on a stage. In Greek theater, bad people acted like good people, good people acted like bad people, and men acted like women (since women weren't allowed to act on stage in those days). Performing on stage, men pretended to be someone they weren't. That's what a lot of this generation has seen in church. Men pretending to be someone they are not. Many in this generation have been raised in churches that disobey or downplay the commands of Scripture. The high ethical standards Jesus requires of his disciples have not been maintained and church members are not held accountable. If the church is filled with hypocrisy, it is hard to blame Bill Gates or anyone else for wanting to be somewhere else on Sunday morning.

So how do you respond when you invite someone to investigate the claims of Christ and they summarily dismiss those claims with the charge that the Christian church is full of hypocrites? Depending on the one who is making the charge, I might counter with four different responses.

Four Possible Responses to the Hypocrisy Argument

1. *Even if the church is full of hypocrites, that doesn't mean the Christian message is false.* When someone rejects Christ based on the hypocrisy argument, he is committing several logical fallacies. When someone attacks the person they are arguing rather than their argument, they are committing the *ad hominem* (to the man) fallacy. By discrediting your church, they hope to undermine the arguments you are making for the gospel. Of course, there have been scandalous figures in many churches through the years, but when someone ignores your presentation of the gospel because he links you to them, he is committing the *guilt-by-association* fallacy. And

when they dodge the implications of the resurrection of Jesus by playing the hypocrisy card, they are throwing up a *red herring* fallacy to distract everyone from the main issue.

Suppose you go for your annual check-up and your doctor walks into the examination room. He is obviously overweight, he is red from a sunburn, alcohol is on his breath from the margaritas he had at lunch, and there is a cigarette dangling from his lips. Then he proceeds to tell you that in order for you to regain your health, you need to lose weight, use sunscreen, stop drinking, and quit smoking. The fact that he doesn't practice what he preaches doesn't mean his message is false. In fact, his message is absolutely true, regardless of how he acts.

2. *Every follower of Jesus Christ is at various stages of growth, so even the most healthy churches have immature believers.* One of the many things that make the gospel such good news is that it is for everyone. No matter what you have done or the lifestyle you have lived, if you repent and trust Christ, he will not turn you away. As a result, many people enter the church with a past full of corruption and vice. These baby believers have a long way to go in the process of sanctification, but if you think they don't look much like Jesus right now, you should have seen them last year! Unbelievers may notice these immature believers in the church and conclude they are hypocrites, but the church has always been a place where broken people come to be mended.

3. *I can't speak for every church, but I can speak for mine. Is there anyone in my church whose hypocrisy is keeping you from seriously considering the claims of Christ?* At this point, I am calling their bluff. I promise them that if they can give me the name of someone in my church, I will call the hypocrite that very day and arrange a meeting where I can explain to them how their behavior is hurting the testimony of our church. If this church member repents, I will ask him to go to my unbelieving friend and seek his forgiveness. If he does not repent, he will be removed from the church until he does. So far, none of my unbelieving friends have been able to give me the specific name of a hypocrite.

4. *You know what? You're right. The church is full of hypocrites. Sometimes, I'm one of them, but let me explain to you why some churches have more and bigger hypocrites than others.* If he is an honest inquirer and really wants to understand, he may give me enough time to talk to him about the three main reasons why I believe the church is full of hypocrites.

Three Reasons Why the Church is Full of Hypocrites

*1. The church ignores "the priesthood of all believers."*Along with the five *solas*, the Reformers recovered another important doctrine that had been abandoned over time. The doctrine of the priesthood of all believers recognizes that with the sacrifice of Christ on the cross, the purpose of the Old Testament priesthood was fulfilled. To confirm this truth, God tore the curtain in the temple that separated the Holy Place from the Holy of Holies from top to bottom. Only the High Priest could enter the Holy Place, where the Ark of the Covenant was kept, and then only once a year on the Day of Atonement. By tearing the curtain, God was communicating that Jesus is our "great high priest" (Heb 4:14) and he holds this position forever. Jesus is the only "mediator between God and men" (1 Tim 2:5). Now anyone can come to God through Christ, without any human mediator. Every believer has direct access to God through Jesus.

There is no office of "priest" in the New Testament church.[5] That is because all believers are priests. Jesus has made the church "a kingdom, priests to his God and Father" (Rev 1:6). As the family of God we are "a chosen race, a royal priesthood" (1 Pet 2:9). Therefore, all of us have a "ministry of reconciliation" (2 Cor 5:18) in which we come between sinners and God in an effort to bring them together by introducing the sinner to Jesus, the great high priest.

As priests, every member of the church is a minister (Eph 4:11–12). Every member is called and gifted to serve in the church. Paul compared the church to the human body. Each member of the church is like a member of that body and everyone has specific roles and abilities. Every member is needed and important even if some are not as visible as others. Eyes are important, but so are ACLs, and many a man has kissed a career in the NFL goodbye because he tore one. ACLs are hidden from view but perform a crucial service. If one member of the body decides not to function, the whole body is affected. If one member tries to do a job he is not called or gifted to do, the body does not function as it should. When every member is in his or her place, playing the right position, the church runs smoothly (1 Cor 12).

What does this have to do with hypocrisy? When you discover your spiritual gift and use it in service to others, several good things will happen. You will grow and mature. For example, if your gift is teaching and you

---

5. The two offices of the church mentioned in the New Testament are elder (sometimes called overseer or pastor) and deacon (e.g., Phil 1:1; 1 Tim 3:2, 8).

use that gift in the church, you will find that you will always learn more than your students as you prepare to teach. Also you will have greater sense of ownership in the church's mission. When you know you are wanted, needed, and playing an important role, you have "skin in the game." For example, if your gift is evangelism and you love inviting your unbelieving friends to church, you will become more zealous about protecting the church's reputation and tamping down hypocrisy.

By the sixteenth century, the church had forgotten this important doctrine and made a false division between the *sacred* and the *secular*. Priests and popes were charged with sacred and "more important" duties like conducting worship services, studying theology, and praying, while farmers and merchants were limited to secular and "less important" endeavors like raising crops and getting them to market. This led to a division in the church between clergy and laity. Ministry was reserved only for the clerical experts while the laity was expected to pay for their services.

This false dichotomy led Martin Luther to protest that "we are all equally priests, as many of us as are baptized,"[6] and one of the first things he did to bring a remedy was translate the Bible into German so the laity could read it like good priests should.

2. *The church tolerates unqualified leaders.* The priesthood of all believers is a doctrine that can be easily abused. This doctrine does not mean that a believer is his own priest and doesn't need the church. It does not mean that every believer's interpretation of Scripture is equal. And it does not mean that there are no offices in the church that have authority over other members.

In fact, there are two main offices in the church. The first is the office of elder. These men lead the church family as older brothers in the Lord. They function as shepherds and so they are sometimes called pastors or overseers. Elders are accountable to Jesus, the Chief Shepherd, and have the authority to provide servant-leadership for the church, guarding sound doctrine and protecting the unity of the church. Each local church normally has several elders who serve in a council (1 Tim 4:14) and when elders are referenced in the New Testament letters it is always in the plural, suggesting shared leadership at each church (Titus 1:5). The council of elders seems to be made up of *ruling elders* who focus on enforcing the Word and *teaching elders* who focus on teaching the Word (1 Tim 5:17).

The second office is that of deacon, which means servant. Acts 6 describes the prototype for deacons and elders. Deacons focus on meeting

6. Luther, *De captivitate*, 283–84.

the material and physical needs of the church family so that the elders can focus on the spiritual and doctrinal needs of the church family. While elders are required to guard the creeds of the church, deacons are required to guard the credibility of the church by taking care of widows and the poor in the church family (Acts 6:1–7). The distinction of these two offices is clear in Paul's address to the Philippians: "to all the saints in Christ Jesus who are at Philippi, with the overseers and deacons" (Phil 1:1).

The men who hold these offices are invested with great authority and power that they are to exercise in service to others. Like Jesus, they must take on the role of a servant, not using their office to be served, but to serve. Elders who serve well will be rewarded by the Chief Shepherd, but elders who abuse their office can expect to be held accountable (1 Pet 5:2–4). Because these offices are endowed with such great authority, they should not be given to just anyone.

The qualifications for both of these offices are very high. Paul spells out these character prerequisites in 1 Timothy 3:1–13 and Titus 1:5–9, and they fall into seven main categories:

Marital Fidelity	He is faithful to keep his wedding vows to his wife, providing in his marriage a picture to the world of Christ's love for us.
Sexual Purity	He abstains from unholy sex (sex before marriage, outside of marriage, and with members of the same sex, and he does not cultivate thoughts of unholy sex).
Family Priority	His dependent children are well-behaved, respectful, under control, and in church.
Financial Accountability	He makes money honorably, saves money wisely, gives money generously, and lives within his means. He pays his bills on time and has a good reputation with customers, clients, creditors, patients, vendors, and even competitors for being reliable and producing quality workmanship.

Doctrinal Integrity	He boldly and clearly articulates and defends the Christian faith. He is biblically literate and able to bring the Bible to bear on every counseling situation.
Emotional Stability	He responds appropriately, even to difficult people. He can manage his anger. While he doesn't enjoy conflict, neither does he avoid it. He doesn't start fights in the church, but he is strong enough to end them by intervening as a peacemaker.
Physical Durability	He can say no to his appetite for food, alcohol, drugs, and laziness. He understands his body belongs to God and his health is a stewardship for which he is accountable.

What does this have to do with hypocrisy in the church? As the old saying goes, "A fish rots from the head down." An organization with a corrupt leadership is doomed to see corruption seep into every rank. The best leaders lead by example and God wants men in these positions who give a good model to the church and the world of what it means to be a Christian. While the church must tolerate immaturity in its ranks as new believers come into the family, the church must never tolerate immaturity in its officers. As leaders, they serve as spokesmen for the church to a skeptical world. Only spiritually mature men can do what must be done to keep hypocrisy in the church to a minimum.

3. *The church neglects church discipline.* The church in Corinth had a massive hypocrisy problem. Among other things, one of its members was sleeping with his father's wife. Besides the "yuck factor" this was an ethical breach that even pagans saw as scandalous. Yet the Corinthian church prided itself on its tolerance of diverse lifestyles and the church leaders did nothing about it. Consequently, the immoral man thought he could have it both ways: flagrantly disobey Jesus but continue to enjoy the privileges of church membership.

The apostle Paul was having none of it. What was his remedy? Give the man a clear choice: Either he could have his sin or he could have the church, but he couldn't have both. If after being confronted he refused to repent, he was to be removed from the fellowship of the church. He couldn't participate in the Lord's Supper. He couldn't serve in any position in the church. He couldn't vote on the church's direction. He couldn't speak in any of the meetings. He could not enjoy church life again until he repented (1 Cor 5:1–13).

This discipline accomplished three things. First, it gave the wayward man his best hope of coming back to God. The pain of being excommunicated was designed to provoke him to change. This tough love was the most likely catalyst to compel him to repent from a decision that was harming him and other people. Second, it sent a message to the rest of the church that these things will not be tolerated. If allowed uncontested, other Christians would be encouraged to sin, thinking there would be no consequences. Third, it took away one more reason for the world to rest on the flimsy excuse that "the church is full of hypocrites."

Every church in every generation has had a problem with hypocrisy. True, only logical fallacies can lead people to summarily dismiss the claims of the church on the basis of hypocrisy in its midst. It is understandable that unbelievers are not even willing to consider those claims when they witness the hypocrisy. For our own good and God's own glory, we must keep order in the ranks and take steps to keep hypocrisy to a minimum. If every church was populated by people who believed they were priests and led by qualified officers who insisted that its members follow Jesus' instruction in Matthew 18:15–20, the church would be purer, hypocrites would be fewer, the church would grow larger, and the gospel would be clearer to a lost and dying world.[7]

---

7. It may seem counterintuitive that church discipline would help the church grow. In the short term, the church may shrink, but the pruning effect would produce health in the long-term, and healthy organisms tend to grow. In the words of Jonathan Edwards in 1737, "And this by the way answers another objection, which some have made, viz. That the way I plead for tends to keep the church of Christ small, and hinder the growth of it. Whereas, I think the contrary tends to keep it small, as it is the wickedness of its members, that above all things in the world prejudices mankind against it; and is the chief stumbling block that hinders the propagation of Christianity; and so the growth of the Christian church. But holiness would cause the light of the church to shine so as to induce others to resort to it" (Edwards, *Ecclesiastical Writings*, 309).

--------------- Things to Know ---------------

– What are the 3 reasons that explain why the church is full of hypocrites?

– What are the 2 offices of the church?

– What are the 7 qualifications of leadership in the church?

— Conclusion —

The Courage of This Generation

I think different religions are different doors to the same house. Sometimes I think the house exists, and sometimes I don't.

−STEVE JOBS, CO-FOUNDER OF APPLE INC.[1]

For the one is called the church militant, the other the church triumphant. The former still wages war on earth, and fights against the flesh, the world, and the prince of this world, the devil; against sin and death. But the latter, having been now discharged, triumphs in heaven immediately after having overcome all those things and rejoices before the Lord. Notwithstanding both have fellow-ship and union one with another.

−THE SECOND HELVETIC CONFESSION, 1566[2]

IN THE END, CAMPING in the snow proved to be worth it.

It's hard to imagine any American soldier who fought at Trenton reflecting on that day with regret. None would later wish he had deserted on Christmas Eve. As decades mellowed the memories, the snow didn't seem so cold, the wind didn't seem so harsh, the sleepless nights didn't seem so dark. In the warm glow of fond reflection, that man had something that no one could take away. He was there when his country needed him. In a time that tried men's souls, he stood the test.

The Battle of Trenton proved to be one of the most pivotal battles of all time. In his best-selling book, *1776*, David McCullough, the Pulitzer Prize winning author, writes,

1. Isaacson, *Steve Jobs.* 15.

2. 17:3.

From the last week of August to the last week of December, the year 1776 had been as dark a time as those devoted to the American cause had ever known—indeed, as dark a time as any in the history of the country. And suddenly, miraculously it seemed, that had changed because of a small band of determined men and their leader. A century later, Sir Otto Trevelyan would write in a classic study of the American Revolution, "It may be doubted whether so small a number of men ever employed so short a space of time with greater and more lasting effects upon the history of the world."[3]

When I first read those words, all I could think of were the men who had deserted. Hours, days, or weeks before Christmas Day, 1776, they made a choice that would haunt them the rest of their lives. The summer soldiers silently slipped away to the soft warmth of hearth and home. The sunshine patriots ran from the fight to join the bulging ranks of spectators.

And then, the news came. A breathless rider galloped into town on a lathered horse: "Washington and the Continental Army have crossed the Delaware and captured Trenton!" A painful mixture of sorrow and regret filled the veteran's heart. "I should have been there," he thought to himself. "I should have been there."

By the time the young soldier was an old man, he had spent years avoiding the subject. He didn't talk about his experience in the war, and many interpreted his silence as humility. Every few years, word would get around that he was a veteran, that he had worn the uniform of the Continental Army. On the Fourth of July, curious boys and admiring men would eventually ask, "You fought with Washington? Tell us! What was it like? What was it like . . . at Trenton?"

Let's be clear. Jesus is building his church and the gates of hell will not prevail against it. He will be victorious and the enemy will be defeated. If you belong to Christ, you are called to join the battle and "take up the whole armor of God, that you may be able to withstand in the evil day, and having done all, to stand firm" (Eph 6:13). This book introduces seven core doctrines that every man needs to master in order to meaningfully join the battle, but God is not depending on you to know, practice, and invest these seven things in the next generation. God depends on no one. The job will get done, with you or without you.

I'll close this book by saying something that might sound like an intentional exaggeration made for dramatic effect. But it is not. It comes from

3. McCullough, *1776*, 290.

years of reflection on the history of the church in America. As I look at the trajectory and velocity of change in our culture, I believe that *there is no generation of Christians in American history that has been called on to display more courage than this rising generation.* Our culture has never been more resistant, our critics have never been more vocal, our enemies have never been more hostile. The need for credible men has never been more urgent—men who will firmly stand against the culture, skillfully answer our critics, and sacrificially love our enemies.

Jesus did not say, "I *might* build my church" or "I *hope* I build my church." He said, "I *will* build my church." Our sovereign God holds the nations in his hand. Since Jesus promised to build his church, kingdoms, empires, and nations have risen and fallen. Caesars, kings, and presidents have come and gone. Two thousand years later, there still remains "a Church on the earth to worship God according to His will."[4] And one day his church will be fully and finally victorious. On that day, what will you wish you had done?

Jesus is coming again to judge the living and the dead. In the meantime, "Brothers, stand firm!"

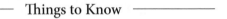

———————— Things to Know ————————

- Take a moment to scan the appendix to review the list of 176 specific things you have come to know in this study.

---

4. Westminster Confession of Faith (1646), Chapter 25.

Bibliography

Alcorn, Randy. *If God is Good: Faith in the Midst of Suffering and Evil*. Colorado Springs: Multnomah, 2009.

Amelia, Simone. "Katy Perry, Lady Gaga, and Jessica Simpson! Christian Girls Gone Wild." *Dr Jays*, June 16, 2011. No pages. Online: http://live.drjays.com/index. php/2011/06/16/katy-perry-lady-gaga-jessica-simpson-christian-girls-gone-wild/.

Armstrong, Lance with Sally Jenkins. *It's Not about the Bike: My Journey Back to Life*. New York: Berkley, 2000.

Augustine, Saint, Bishop of Hippo. *Confessions and Enchiridion*, translated and edited by Albert C. Outler. Philadelphia: Westminster, 1955. No pages. Online: http://www. ccel.org/ccel/augustine/confessions.iv.html.

Barna Group. "Spirituality May Be Hot in America, But 76 Million Adults Never Attend Church." *Barna*, 2009. No pages. Online: http://www.barna.org/barna-update/ article/5-barna-update/158-spirituality-may-be-hot-in-america-but-76-million-adults-never-attend-church.

Barrick, Audrey. "Rob Bell Gets Evangelicals Talking About Hell," *The Christian Post*, March 2, 2011. No pages. Online: http://www.christianpost.com/news/rob-bell-gets-evangelicals-talking-about-hell-49255/.

Bateman, Steve. *Which "Real" Jesus?: Jonathan Edwards, Benjamin Franklin, and the Early American Roots of the Current Debate*. Eugene, OR: Wipf and Stock, 2008.

Bell, Rob. *Love Wins: A Book About Heaven, Hell, and the Fate of Every Person Who Ever Lived*. New York: Harper One, 2011.

Biskupic, Joan. *American Original: The Life and Constitution of Supreme Court Justice Antonin Scalia*. New York: Sarah Crichton, 2009.

Book of Concord: The Confessions of the Lutheran Concord. The Larger Catechism. No pages. Online: http://bookofconcord.org/lc-4-creed.php.

Bruce, Robert, and Debra Fulghum Bruce. *Becoming Spiritual Soulmates with Your Child*. Nashville: Broadman & Holman, 1996.

Calmes, Jackie. "Obama Says Same-Sex Marriage Should Be Legal." *New York Times,* May 9, 2012. No pages. Online: http://www.nytimes.com/2012/05/10/us/politics/obama-says-same-sex-marriage-should-be-legal.html?_r=0.

Calvin, John. *Calvin's Commentaries*. Translated by John Pringle and William Pringle. 23 vols. Reprint, Grand Rapids: Baker, 1993.

Calvin, John. *Institutes of the Christian Religion*. Translated by Ford Lewis Battles. Edited by John T. McNeill. 2 vols. Philadelphia: Westminster, 1960.

Chumley, Cheryl. "Michael Bloomberg: I've 'earned my place in heaven' for anti-gun crusade." *The Washington Times*, April 16, 2014. Online: http://www.washingtontimes. com/news/2014/apr/16/michael-bloomberg-ive-earned-my-place-in-heaven-fo/.

The Church of Jesus Christ of Latter Days Saints. "Pre-Earth Life." *Latter Day Saints*, 2012. No pages. Online: https://www.lds.org/topics/pre-earth-life?lang=eng.

Clabough, Raven. "Bill Mahr Lashes Out At the Bible." *The New American*, October 1, 2010. No pages. Online: http://www.thenewamerican.com/usnews/politics/item/3384-bill-maher-lashes-out-against-bible.

Coles, Robert and Geoffrey Stokes. *Sex and the American Teenager*. New York: Harper and Row, 1985.

Dean, Kenda Creasy. *Almost Christian: What the Faith of Our Teenagers Is Telling the American Church*. Oxford: Oxford University Press, 2010.

Doyle, Arthur Conan. *The Memoirs of Sherlock Holmes*. New York: Oxford University Press, 1993.

Dyck, Drew. *Generation Ex-Christian: Why Young Adults Are Leaving the Faith . . . and How to Bring Them Back*. Chicago: Moody, 2010.

Edwards, Jonathan. *Ecclesiastical Writings*. Vol. 12 of *The Works of Jonathan Edwards*. Edited by David Hall. New Haven, CT: Yale University Press, 1994.

Edwards, Jonathan. *The Works of Jonathan Edwards*. Revised and edited by Edward Hickman. 2 vols. London, 1834. Reprint, Edinburgh: Banner of Truth Trust, 1988.

Ehrman, Bart D. *Jesus, Interrupted: Revealing the Hidden Contradictions in the Bible (and Why We Don't Know About Them)*. New York: Harper Collins, 2009.

Foust, Michael. "Obama: Sin is what doesn't match 'my values.'" *Baptist Press*, March 2, 2012. No pages. Online: http://www.bpnews.net/bpnews.asp?id=37310.

George, Timothy. *Is the Father of Jesus the God of Muhammed? Understanding the Differences Between Christianity and Islam*. Grand Rapids: Zondervan, 2002.

Gerstner, John H. *A Primer on Justification*. Phillipsburg, NJ: Presbyterian and Reformed Publishing, 1983.

Grudem, Wayne. *Systematic Theology: An Introduction to Biblical Doctrine*. Grand Rapids: Zondervan, 1994.

Hall, Nicole. "Are There Really More Mobile Phones Than Toothbrushes?" *The 60 Second Marketer*. No pages. Online: http://60secondmarketer.com/blog/2011/10/18/more-mobile-phones-than-toothbrushes/.

Harris, Sam. *Letter to a Christian Nation*. New York: Alfred A. Knopf, 2006.

Hinch, Jim. "Where Are the People?" *The American Scholar*, Winter 2014. No pages. Online: http://theamericanscholar.org/where-are-the-people/#.UtFmMqnGLXA.

Hoffman, Claire. "Katy Conquers All." *Marie Claire*, December 9, 2013. No pages. Online: http://www.marieclaire.com/celebrity-lifestyle/celebrities/katy-perry-feature-katheryn-hudson.

Horton, Michael. *The Gospel-Driven Life: Being Good News People in a Bad News World*. Grand Rapids: Baker, 2009.

Hunt, Susan. *Heirs of the Covenant: Leaving a Legacy of Faith for the Next Generation*. Wheaton: Crossway Books, 1998.

Isaacson, Walter. "In Search of the Real Bill Gates." *Time Magazine*, January 13, 1997. No pages. Online: http://content.time.com/time/magazine/article/0,9171,1120657,00.html.

Isaacson, Walter. *Steve Jobs*. New York: Simon and Schuster, 2011.

Kelly, Mark. "Study: Unchurched Americans Turned Off By Church, Open to Christians." *Lifeway*, January 9, 2008. No pages. Online: http://www.lifeway.com/Article/LifeWay-Research-finds-unchurched-Americans-turned-off-by-church-open-to-Christians.

Killough, Ashley. "Osteen: Romney is a Christian." CNN, April 24, 2012. No pages. Online: http://politicalticker.blogs.cnn.com/2012/04/24/osteen-romney-is-a-christian/.

BIBLIOGRAPHY

Koran. 5th rev. ed. Translated by N.J. Daewood. New York: Penguin Classics, 1999.

Leclaire, Jennifer. "Oprah Winfrey: 'I Am A Christian.'" *CharismaNews*, April 26, 2012. No pages. Online: http://www.charismanews.com/us/33290-oprah-winfrey-i-am-a-christian.

Lenhart, Amanda. "Teens, Smartphones, and Texting." PewResearch Internet Project. March 19, 2012. http://www.pewinternet.org/2012/03/19/teens-smartphones-texting/.

Lesinski, Jeanne M. *Bill Gates*. Minneapolis: Twenty-First Century Books, 1997.

Lewis, C.S. *Mere Christianity*. New York: MacMillan, 1943.

Lindsell, Harold. *The Battle for the Bible*. Grand Rapids: Zondervan, 1976.

Lofton, John. "Warren Buffet 'Agnostic,' Bill Gates Rejects Sermon on the Mount, Not 'Huge Believer' in 'Specific Elements' of Christianity." *The American View*, 2006. No pages. Online: http://archive.theamericanview.com/index.php?id=649.

Low, Robbie. "The Truth about Men and Church." *Touchstone*, June 2003. No pages. Online: http://www.touchstonemag.com/archives/article.php?id=16-05-024-v.

Luther, Martin. "Instructions to the Perplexed and Doubting, to George Spenlein, April 8, 1516." In *Luther: Letters of Spiritual Counsel*, translated by Theodore G. Tappert. Library of Christian Classics, Vol. 18. Quoted in "Martin Luther and the Great Exchange." *Post Barthian*, March 28, 2012. No pages. Online: http://postbarthian.com/2012/03/28/martin-luther-and-the-great-exchange/.

Luther, Martin. *De captivitate Babylonica ecclesiae praeludium* [*Prelude Concerning the Babylonian Captivity of the Church*], Weimar Ausgabe 6, 564.6–14. Quoted in Norman Nagel, "Luther and the Priesthood of All Believers," *Concordia Theological Quarterly* 61, no. 4 (October 1997) 283–84.

Manson, Marilyn. Interview by Bill Maher, *Politically Incorrect*, August 13, 1997. Online: http://www.mansonwiki.com/wiki/Interview:1997/08/13_Politically_Incorrect.

Maraniss, David. *When Pride Still Mattered: A Life of Vince Lombardi*. New York: Simon and Schuster, 1999.

Marikar, Sheila. "Brad Pitt and More Stars Go Back on Christian Beliefs." ABC News, May 19, 2011. No pages. Online: http://abcnews.go.com/Entertainment/brad-pitt-katy-perry-back-christian beliefs/story?id=13620940#.TowrV1HGJG8.

McCullough, David. *1776*. New York: Simon and Schuster, 2005.

McGrath, Alister. *"I Believe: Exploring the Apostles' Creed."* Downers Grove: Intervarsity Press, 1997.

McKay, Holley "Pop Tarts: Miley Cyrus: 'Faith keeps me grounded." Foxnews.com, March 28, 2008. No pages. Online: http://www.foxnews.com/story/2008/03/28/pop-tarts-miley-cyrus-faith-keeps-me-grounded/.

McQuilkin, Robertson. *Understanding and Applying the Bible*. Chicago: Moody, 1992.

Morgan, Fiona. "Complete Interview with Bart Ehrman." *Indy Week*, March 25, 2009. No pages. Online: http://www.indyweek.com/indyweek/complete-interview-with-bart-ehrman/Content?oid=1214629.

Murrow, David. *Why Men Hate Going to Church*. Nashville: Thomas Nelson, 2005.

Nagel, Norman. "Luther and the Priesthood of All Believers." *Concordia Theological Quarterly* 61, no. 4 (October 1997) 283-84.

Newport, Frank. "Americans' Church Attendance Inches Up in 2010." *Gallup Well-Being*, June 25, 2010. No pages. Online: http://www.gallup.com/poll/141044/americans-church-attendance-inches-2010.aspx.

———. "In U.S., 77% Identify as Christians." *Gallup Politics,* December 24, 2012. No pages. Online: http://www.gallup.com/poll/159548/identify-christian.aspx.

Nord, Christine Winquist and Jerry West. "Fathers' and Mothers' Involvement in Their Children's Schools by Family Type and Resident Status." Washington, DC: U.S. Dept of Education, National Center of Education Statistics, 2001. Online: http://nces.ed.gov/pubs2001/2001032.pdf.

NPR, "Bart Ehrman, Questioning Religion on Why We Suffer." The Richard Dawkins Foundation, February 18, 2008. No pages. Online: http://richarddawkins.net/audio/2286-bart-ehrman-questioning-religion-on-why-we-suffer.

Packer, J. I. and Gary A. Parrett. *Grounded in the Gospel: Building Believers the Old-Fashioned Way.* Grand Rapids: Baker, 2010.

Paine, Thomas. "The American Crisis." In *Our Nation's Archives: The History of the United States in Documents,* 135–36. Edited by Erik Bruun and Jay Crosby. New York: Back Dog and Leventhal, 1999.

Pascal, Blaise. *Pensees (#425).* Translated by W. F. Trotter. New York: E.P. Dutton and Co., 1958. http://oregonstate.edu/instruct/phl302/texts/pascal/pensees-contents.html.

Pearson, Ryan. "Q&A: Snoop Dogg on Ccriticism, Religion, Reggae CD." Associated Press, March 14, 2013. No pages. Online: http://music.yahoo.com/news/q-snoop-dogg-criticism-religion-reggae-cd-132036617.html.

Pelikan, Jaroslav and Valerie R. Hotchkiss, eds. *Creeds and Confessions of Faith in the Christian Tradition,* 3 vols. New Haven: Yale University Press, 2003.

Piper, John. *Desiring God: Meditations of a Christian Hedonist.* Expanded edition. Sisters, OR: Multnomah, 1996.

Piper, John. *Think: The Life of the Mind and the Love of God.* Wheaton: Crossway, 2010.

Rankin, Russ. "Survey: One in Five Americans Undecided About Easter Attendance." Lifeway. No pages. Online: http://www.lifeway.com/Article/research-survey-one-in-five-americans-undecided-about-easter-church-attendance?CARID=jdw-032613.

Regnerus, Mark. "The Case for Early Marriage," *Christianity Today,* July 31, 2009. No pages. Online: http://www.christianitytoday.com/ct/2009/august/16.22.html.

Reilly, Rick. "Let us Pray [strikethrough] Play." *Sports Illustrated,* April 26, 2004. No pages. Online: http://www.sportsillustrated.com/vault/article/magazine/MAG1031905/index.htm.

Robinson, Gene. *God Believes in Love: Straight Talk About Gay Marriage.* New York: Alfred A. Knopf, 2012.

Sanneh, Kelefa. "Savoring a Moment in the Sun, Despite a Court Date." *New York Times,* February 26, 2008. No pages. Online: http://www.nytimes.com/2008/02/26/arts/music/26wayn.html?_r=4&oref=slogin&oref=slogin.

Smith, Aaron. "Americans and Text Messaging." PewResearch Internet Project, September 19, 2011. http://www.pewinternet.org/2011/09/19/americans-and-text-messaging/.

Smith, Christian with Patricia Snell. *Souls in Transition: The Religious and Spiritual Lives of Emerging Adults.* Oxford: Oxford University Press, 2009.

Sproul, R.C. *Chosen by God.* Wheaton: Tyndale House, 1987.

———. *Not a Chance: The Myth of Chance in Modern Science and Cosmology.* Grand Rapids: Baker Books, 1994.

Stott, John W. *The Cross of Christ.* Downers Grove: Intervarsity Press, 1986.

Twain, Mark. *The Wit and Wisdom of Mark Twain.* Edited by Alex Ayres. New York: Meridan, 1987.

Wachlin, Marie. "What do American teens need to know and what do they know?" In *The Bible Literacy Report: What do American Teens Need to Know and What Do They Know?*, 8–21. New York: Bible Literacy Project, 2005. Online: http://www. bibleliteracy.org/secure/documents/bibleliteracyreport2005.pdf.

Waite, Linda J. and Maggie Gallagher. *The Case for Marriage: Why Married People are Happier, Healthier, and Better Off Financially.* New York: Broadway Books, 2000.

Wallis, Jim. "The Truth Smirks." *Sojourners,* July 2009. No pages. Online: http://sojo.net/ magazine/2009/07/truth-smirks.

Watson, Thomas. *A Body of Divinity: Contained in Sermons Upon the Westminster Assembly's Catechism.* Los Angeles: Indo-European Publishing, 2011.

WENN, "Simpson Shies Away From Christian Roots." Contactmusic.com, September 6, 2005. No pages. Online: http://www.contactmusic.com/news-article/simpson-shies-away-from-christian-roots.

— Appendix —
176 Things Every Man Should Know

MEN GENERALLY LIKE TO count, measure, and record things. We need fixed, objective goals. Hard targets. It's difficult for us to work on a project or play a game without keeping some kind of score. If you learn all the things at the end of each chapter of this book, you will know 176 vital things that every Christian man should know. Of course, knowing these things is not enough. We must also practice these things and invest them in the next generation. But you cannot pass on what you do not possess. Before you can invest these things, you have to know them. So here's your challenge. Test yourself. How much do you know?

The 1st Thing: How to Glorify God–The Purpose

- What are the 4 ways this generation is departing from the historic Christian faith?

- What are the 2 greatest predictors that your children will hold to the Christian faith?

- What are the 2 obstacles to credibility?

- What are the 2 components of credibility?

- What are the 2 senses in which the Bible speaks of the "glory of God"?

- What are the 4 ways we glorify God in our relationship with Jesus?

The 2nd Thing: How to Listen to God–The Bible

- What are the 2 kinds of revelation?

- What are the 66 books of the Bible?

- What are the 3 standards of the New Testament canon?

- What are the 7 rules of interpretation?

The 3rd Thing: How to Think About God–The Creed

- What are the 2 things every Christian man ought to know about creeds?
- What are the 3 chief articles of the Apostles' Creed?
- What are the 4 reconcilable facts of the doctrine of the trinity?

The 4th Thing: How to Please God–The Law

- What are the 3 kinds of law?
- What are the 10 Commandments?
- What are the 3 abuses of the Law?
- What are the 2 summaries of the law?
- What are the 3 uses of the law?

The 5th Thing: How to Be Reconciled to God–The Gospel

- What are the 3 tenses of salvation?
- What are the 3 facets of salvation?
- What are the 4 elements of the gospel?
- What are the 5 slogans of the Reformation?
- What are the 3 great imputations?

The 6th Thing: How to Talk to God–The Prayer

- What are the 2 places to pray?
- What are the 6 petitions of the Lord's Prayer?

The 7th Thing: How to Serve God–The Church

- What are the 8 meanings of the word "church"?
- What are the 3 marks of a true church?
- What are the 2 sacraments (or ordinances) of the church?

– What are the 3 purposes of the church?

– What are the 3 reasons that explain why the church is full of hypocrites?

– What are the 2 offices of the church?

– What are the 7 qualifications of leadership in the church?